EVERYONE WINS!

How You Can Enhance and Optimize Business Relationships Just Like Ultra-Wealthy Entrepreneurs

RUSS ALAN PRINCE

FRANK V. CARONE

JOHN J. BOWEN JR.

FOREWORD BY DAN SULLIVAN

DISCLAIMER

This material is intended to be used for educational purposes only and does not constitute a solicitation to purchase any security or advisory services.

Everyone Wins!

How You Can Enhance and Optimize Business Relationships Just Like Ultra-Wealthy Entrepreneurs

By Russ Alan Prince, Frank V. Carone and John J. Bowen Jr.

To Sandi—

Because being married to me tests her patience daily.

Love, Russ

To my wife Diana, daughter Gabriella and son Francesco.
And of course our family members no longer
with us whose sacrifices paved the way.

—Frank

To my wife, Jeanne—as always, it's my privilege to share
my business, my life and my love with you.

—John

Table of Contents

PART III

CODA

APPENDICES

Foreword

Over the past four decades that I've spent helping entrepreneurs grow and thrive, I've learned that one of the best ways to succeed in business dealings—with staff, partners, people with whom you're negotiating and others—is to make it all about them. When your focus is deeply on the person or people in front of you, you actually put yourself in the best possible position to walk away with the results you most want for you and your company.

That's essentially what this book is all about—how to come out of business situations as a winner largely by making sure the people around you are also winners. Instead of adopting an "I must win, and who cares about you?" attitude, you seek to have everyone emerge victorious.

Indeed, that's exactly what top entrepreneurs seek to do consistently. During their interactions, they put the attention not on themselves but on everyone else in the room. That in turn helps them be very successful. Why? Because it sends a message that they're focused not on how much or how quickly they can get paid but on how they can deliver real value in the situation at hand.

Of course, it can be easy to present yourself as someone who is not worried about money when you're extraordinarily wealthy and successful. But what if you're an entrepreneur who is not so "cash confident"? It's still smart to do the same thing even when you need to close the deal and get that check. It's a fact of life, not just of entrepreneurship, that the world rewards those who don't concentrate on themselves all the time. Think about the ideas of paying attention to others, asking great questions and listening deeply to what they have to tell you so you can add value to their lives. Those skills work in dating, they work in marriage, they work in parenting—and they work in business!

Where you're coming from is that it's always about them and not about you. We can always get our own way if we can just stay out of our way.

Even better: These skills can be learned. You can replace the anxiety you may feel today when entering a negotiation—anxiety that practically radiates off you—with quiet confidence and a sense of freedom that prompt others to want to help you achieve your agenda. Accomplishing that outcome can mean something as little as being able to engage in an hourlong conversation, when you spend the bulk of that time asking great questions to learn how to bring value to the people on the other side of the table!

When you are able to build up that confidence, you can place your attention on other people—artfully gaining deep insights into what really matters to them as well as what causes them concern so you can identify ways to create value together, and you can do so in a way that relaxes and reassures them. This is the basis for your winning and helping them win too.

What's more, it's the basis for all of you winning in bigger ways than you may have thought possible. Did you know that when you ask powerful questions, you actually create a stronger impression on other people than you do by giving a powerful answer to a question they ask you? Being asked a great question will do more to change a person's thinking about a situation, an opportunity or a problem—as well as your potential role in addressing it. Great questioning can help the other person see that you bring more to the table than they thought and that you can offer more value to them than they initially expected.

Those types of revelations and "aha!" moments are exactly what can transform a deal from a short-term, one-off, low-profit transaction to a long-term, strategic, high-value commitment to working with you on a broad range of business issues.

The flip side is also true. Asking great questions and listening deeply to the answers can empower you to clearly see when there is not an opportunity to add value, so you can move on. This is massively important to successful entrepreneurship—knowing when an "opportunity" is really a distraction from what you do best and where you should be focused. But as this book reveals, there are ways to bow out that keep the door open for potentially successful ventures with that person in the future—and even garner introductions and referrals from the person to whom you said no thanks!

Bottom line: The process you're about to discover can be a tremendous tool for differentiating yourself very quickly in a wide variety of business situations, showing you're an entrepreneur who is concerned about creating value and enhancing relationships to benefit everyone. In today's world of never-ending time crunches, simply giving your attention to others and engaging with them can elevate you.

It can also bring a sense of safety to your interactions with others. When the people around you feel safe and know that you are out to create tremendous value with them, they feel relaxed—which in turn makes them more receptive to you, your ideas and your goals. Rather than feel manipulated, they recognize clearly that you are actually looking out for them and considering their best interests along with your own.

Just imagine what you can accomplish together when the people you do business with know that's the place you're coming from!

Dan Sullivan

Dan Sullivan
Founder and President
The Strategic Coach, Inc.

A Rising Tide Lifts All Boats

We wrote this book because we want you to win.

When everyone wins,
you win.

When everyone wins,
you win, now and in the future.

When everyone wins,
you win in ways you weren't even thinking about.

When everyone wins,
you win in your business life as well as your personal life, especially during rough times.

When everyone wins,
you win bigger than you probably imagined you could.

About This Book

Is this book for you? Ask yourself some questions:

Do I want those with whom I have business relationships to do everything in their power to help me make my company as successful as possible?

Do I want to significantly increase my ability to become seriously wealthy so I can take care of the people I love and support the causes that matter to me?

Do I want to get these results while being extremely ethical, without manipulation or deception?

If your answer to these questions is **yes**, then you're in the right place.

We're going to share with you an empirically and experientially validated approach—a proven process—for creating, enhancing and even optimizing powerful business relationships. You can then harness these relationships so they do as much as possible to help you and your company excel.

Why? Business success and business relationships are inextricably connected. In nearly all the cases we have seen (personally and in research), entrepreneurs' accomplishments can be traced back to their business relationships. Yes, some entrepreneurs have industry-disrupting ideas. And yes, some entrepreneurs' sheer brilliance supersedes everything else. However, in extensively researching, observing and working with very successful ultra-wealthy entrepreneurs over two decades, we have discovered that their accomplishments can largely be credited to the quality of their business relationships.

We call this proven process the *Everyone Wins Process* because, as the name suggests, all the people engaged in it come out winning.

In this book, we'll provide you with a foundational understanding of the Everyone Wins Process along with actionable strategies and tools you can implement immediately to start getting results right away.

The Everyone Wins Process has three fundamental characteristics.

Characteristic 1: The Everyone Wins Process is highly ethical

While ethics in business are obstacles for some people, we strongly believe in the importance of avoiding coercion, deception and manipulation. Duplicity and deceit are out of the question.

You probably know a few entrepreneurs for whom winning at all costs is the only answer. For them, the end justifies the means no matter what and no matter who gets hurt. For them, the people who get trampled along the way to victory are irrelevant.

While such an approach can produce substantial results immediately, it leaves bodies in its wake—and has a high likelihood of being self-destructive in the long run. The "win at any cost" mantra often creates a plethora of enemies and leads to eventual ruin.

The Everyone Wins Process is the antithesis of this approach. The absolute best outcome in business situations is when everyone wins, and that is the outcome we feel you must always strive for.

Important: Being ethical in business is a decision. Con artists, grifters, swindlers and others lacking a moral compass can twist and abuse the process in this book to devastate other people. In our experience, however, the unethical use of the Everyone Wins Process tends to spell doom for the unethical entrepreneur.

Characteristic 2: The Everyone Wins Process generates amazing results

If you're anything like the thousands of entrepreneurs we've studied over the past two decades, you want to hit it big.

One of the best ways to exponentially increase your success is to enhance and optimize your business relationships. Skillfully encouraging others—including fellow business owners, employees, government bureaucrats and the professionals you engage with—to consistently make concerted efforts to help you achieve wins is an incredible way to reach your end goals (and even go beyond them).

Consider, for example, ultra-wealthy entrepreneurs (those with a net worth of $30 million or more; See **Appendix A: Researching Ultra-Wealthy Entrepreneurs**). Our research reveals that the most successful members of this group—the best of the best, essentially— usually follow the tenets of the Everyone Wins Process, and the support these entrepreneurs receive from their business associates contributes significantly to their incredible success.

By using the Everyone Wins Process, you build outstanding rapport and greater loyalties that can help you take your business to extreme heights. Even in circumstances that are short term or episodic (such as when you're negotiating the sale of your company), to some degree you can enhance the relationship you have with buyers—resulting in a higher price and better terms.

The Everyone Wins Process can also benefit your overall life beyond your business and your bottom line. For example, the people with whom you build optimal business relationships are also likely to help you in a variety of ways, including when you face personal adversity.

Characteristic 3: The Everyone Wins Process can be learned

The Everyone Wins Process is a tried-and-true methodology for generating outstanding results consistently. There are no magic, secret formulas or hidden knowledge. All you need to masterfully enhance and optimize business relationships is the proper mindset supported by the appropriate skills.

Without a doubt, you can learn and master the Everyone Wins Process. We know because we work with select entrepreneurs to use the Everyone Wins Process to dramatically multiply their net worth (see **Appendix B: Personal Wealth Creation Coaching**).

Even if you already know the mindset and have the skills underlying this process and are using them, you still might be able to get incrementally better at making them work for you. Indeed, we believe all of us can continually improve how we work with and help others in order to achieve our agendas.

Based on researching the business and wealth-building best practices of the most accomplished ultra-wealthy entrepreneurs, we believe that nearly all determined business owners can exponentially accelerate their success by mastering the Everyone Wins Process.

Important: While this process can be learned, it requires your commitment. You have to put in the time and effort to master and continually refine your use of the Everyone Wins Process.

You will notice certain phrases used throughout this primer such as "ultra-wealth," "serious wealth" and "optimal relationships." The purpose is for you to come away with life-changing aspirational goals and to create a significant thought-provoking mindset. Our goal is for you to set your goals beyond what you thought possible prior to reading this book and, in fact, to even scare you a little and, of course, to learn how to go about achieving them. So, enjoy!

Let's start with the first component of the Everyone Wins Process—the proper mindset that you must have to guide your efforts and action steps.

PART I

The Winning Mindset

As a hard-charging entrepreneur, you may want to dive right into the Everyone Wins Process and start using it to generate great results.

We hate to say it, but you need to hit the brakes. The fact is, as with any major new process or system, you'll get the best results with the Everyone Wins Process if you first take a big step back.

Specifically, you need to consider some questions about your business and your own success that you may not have thought about in some time. You may also need to revise some of your long-held assumptions about what it takes to win big in business-related situations.

In the next several chapters, you'll discover how to adopt the ideal mindset and principles that will empower you to use the Everyone Wins Process in ways that can truly maximize your success.

CHAPTER 1

What Is Winning?

When it comes right down to it, winning means different things to different entrepreneurs. Winning can be about business success as well as personal achievements. To start gaining clarity, consider these questions.

When I think about winning, what comes to mind?

When it comes to my business, what does winning mean?

What is winning when I think about personal wealth?

There are no right or wrong responses here. Your answers to these questions are your answers, and they're all that matter. Also, winning is rarely defined in just one way. Most entrepreneurs use a number of criteria to describe what winning looks and feels like to them. The key is to be specific so you gain clarity.

Becoming seriously wealthy

That said, there is one facet of winning that we see shared among most ultra-wealthy entrepreneurs—becoming seriously wealthy.

Among entrepreneurs at all levels of achievement, "amassing a personal fortune" always ranks high as a goal. Entrepreneurship is risky and demands hard work. Not surprisingly, serious personal wealth is typically seen as a key reward of that risk-taking and effort.

For most entrepreneurs, the drive to amass serious wealth goes beyond simply wanting to see a healthy bottom line on the balance sheet. Serious wealth is all about freedom—the freedom to do what they choose. Serious wealth is also about being able to take good care of loved ones as well as support the causes they care about. Some even want to become seriously wealthy so they can positively change the world at large. Entrepreneurs generally feel they are winning when they have the wealth necessary to achieve these and similar outcomes.

Setting your serious wealth goals

When it comes to building serious wealth, you first need to specify how much you want to be worth.

Put another way, what is your *financial end goal*? It could be a few million dollars, a few hundred million or more. Regardless, it's helpful to have a target to aim at—keeping in mind that you'll probably raise the target as you get close to hitting it. A pretty consistent trend among hard-driving entrepreneurs is that once they near their financial end goal, they increase the number—again and again and again.

Regardless of the number you choose, make it a stretch goal—one that feels challenging or even slightly intimidating. All the entrepreneurs we've worked with had lofty financial end goals and reached or exceeded them.

Of course, to achieve your financial end goal, you'll need to take a number of smaller steps along the way. Brainstorm the intermediary goals and accomplishments that will incrementally get you closer and closer to your financial end goal. You want to be able to draw a direct line between your intermediary goals and your financial end goal. This way, your intermediary goals will help keep you on track and result in consistent progress.

The family office option

As an entrepreneur, creating a personal fortune is predicated on your ability to grow your company—which in turn is based largely on your ability to enhance and optimize business relationships. Once you've started to amass some meaningful personal wealth, you can take advantage of a practice often used by the Super Rich (those with a net worth of $500 million or more) and other very successful individuals: having your own family office (see **Appendix C: Your Own Family Office**).

Playing the long game

For top entrepreneurs, winning involves playing "the long game"—following a long-term strategy to get desired results. Business relationships (and often personal relationships) are the cornerstones of ultra-wealthy business owners' success. They generally recognize that their ability to enhance and optimize business relationships takes time.

This focus on the long game differs from what we see among less successful entrepreneurs, most of whom tend to be reactive—looking to take the next immediate action without thinking strategically or considering longer-term implications. They typically respond to changes (in sometimes dramatic ways) as opposed to having well-defined objectives and then developing and following a set of plans to achieve them. In particular, they don't tend to examine their business relationships and think about them in ways that can translate into greater business success and personal wealth.

Most entrepreneurs have a vision of what they want to achieve, but many lack a clear path to follow. They're often not doing a particularly good job of planning their company's (or their own) financial future.

Incidentally, the long-game approach is why grifters who abuse the Everyone Wins Process by exploiting and cheating other people may have some short-term positive results but will very often fail at building successful companies. It's rarely possible for grifters to be duplicitous and still be able to win over and over again as their reputation gets shredded.

So before we start discussing the nature of enhancing and optimizing business relationships, come up with a number that you want to achieve that makes you seriously wealthy—your financial end goal. That number can serve as your North Star as you navigate your business and build relationships that can help you get what you most want.

To gain some more insight into the nature of business relationships—and how you can enhance and optimize them so you come out winning—let's review the business relationship hierarchy.

CHAPTER 2

The Business Relationship Hierarchy

It takes a lot to achieve entrepreneurial success. Hard work, smarts and perseverance are all often essential to building a top-notch business. Similarly, it takes a lot to become seriously wealthy.

But as we noted earlier, whether you generate success in business and build serious wealth largely comes down to the quality of your business relationships and your ability to get more from those relationships. In fact, methodologies such as the Everyone Wins Process are foundational to most effective personal wealth creation coaching programs.

With that in mind, ask yourself the following questions.

Are my business relationships the kinds that make me more successful?

How would things change for me and my company if just about everyone with whom I have a business relationship made an effort to help me excel?

How would other aspects of my life change because my business associates are looking for ways to help me in good times and bad?

The Everyone Wins Process is all about building the best possible business relationships in any situation. The reason top ultra-wealthy entrepreneurs use this type of process is because they seek to powerfully incentivize other people to help them succeed and because they genuinely care about others. Their objectives are to get others to sincerely care about and invest in their success—as well as regularly provide support so they achieve much more than would otherwise be possible.

The good news: **You can do the same**.

When you systematically apply the Everyone Wins Process, you make it easy for people to see why they should help you reach your goals—and often you make it much easier for them to actually provide that help. For example:

- People you meet at conferences may start introducing you to potential customers.

- Potential buyers of your business may be willing to pay you more and offer better terms.

- Your employees may work harder and take it upon themselves to make the company run better.

It all depends on what kind of relationship you want to have with the different people you deal with in business. The choice is yours. You're in control.

The business relationship hierarchy

To better understand your options and the role your business relationships can play in your success, consider the business relationship hierarchy (see

Exhibit 2.1), which summarizes the four levels of relationships you can have with others.

In reviewing this hierarchy, think about your existing business relationships and where they fit today. Also, think about what would happen if you moved them up in the hierarchy to a higher level—especially to the optimal level.

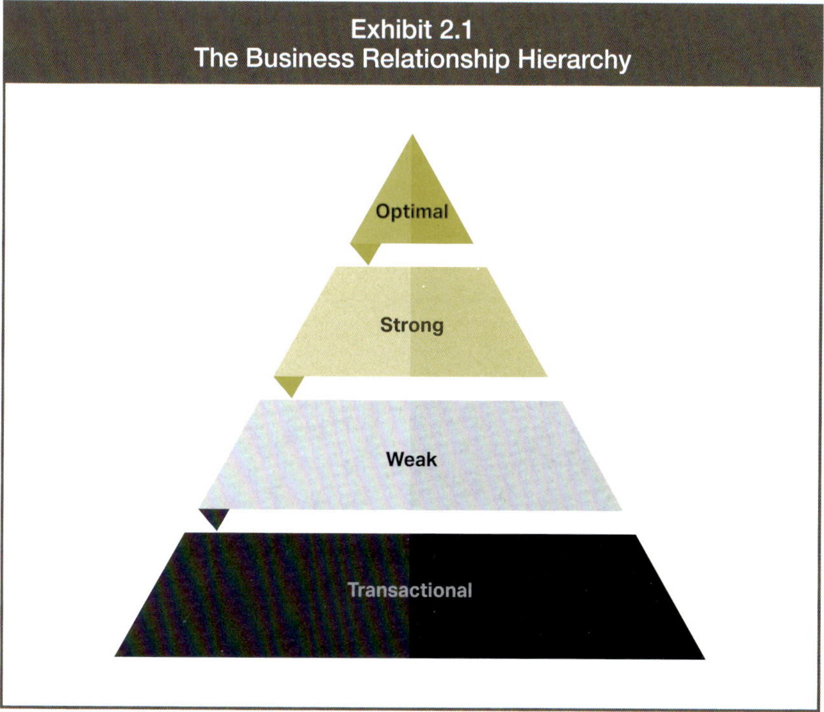

1. Transactional relationships

At the bottom of the hierarchy, transactional relationships permeate all aspects of all our lives. They're ethereal, limited relationships with people we deal with in business contexts. Examples include the driver of the car you hire to get you to the airport or the plumber you hire to fix your heating system.

That said, you can make transactional relationships more advantageous to you. When you do so, the driver may be more polite and responsive, and the plumber may take care of a few minor issues without charging for them.

The upshot: You can choose to enhance any business relationship—even a very limited one. All of your relationships can be strengthened to some degree, depending on the circumstances. The choice of whether to do so is yours.

2. Weak relationships

The next level up is weak relationships. These relationships are with people you deal with in business with whom you have some degree of rapport—you can call on them and they will likely respond.

Weak relationships in business are the norm. You likely know lots and lots of people, but you don't want to get to know them all that well, considering the many tasks you have to get done.

Once again, you can move a weak relationship up in the hierarchy, or you can enhance a weak relationship in a particular situation while keeping that relationship in the weak category. It's your decision.

3. Strong relationships

More intense business relationships are categorized as strong. These are with people you know well. They often make up the business support network you regularly rely on.

Very likely, the people with whom you have strong relationships will be instrumental in helping you grow your company. They also can help you become seriously wealthy.

4. Optimal relationships

At the pinnacle of the business relationship hierarchy are optimal relationships. These relationships might seem almost magical. They are with your "best friends in business"—your inner circle—who are intensely motivated to do whatever they can to help you become more successful.

Important: Because of the time and effort required to establish and maintain optimal relationships, it's only possible to have a handful of them. That's okay—you don't need scores of optimal relationships to achieve tremendous success. The most successful ultra-wealthy entrepreneurs strategically maximize the value of their optimal relationships. And even these powerful relationships can be supercharged when necessary.

Furthermore, we'll say it once again: You can choose to enhance any relationship in any of these four categories. That may mean working to move a relationship into a higher category or simply getting more from a relationship within a particular category.

Getting more

There are distinct advantages to moving your business relationships higher up the hierarchy in terms of your overall success, your reputation and your ability to tap new opportunities. (See **Exhibit 2.2**.) Simply put, as you move relationships up, you receive more benefits.

Exhibit 2.2 Advantages of Moving Up the Business Relationship Hierarchy			
Levels	**Success**	**Your reputation**	**New opportunities**
Optimal	Ongoing and cumulative	Draws people and possibilities to you	Consistent
Strong	Common but intermittent	Solid, leading to more but infrequent opportunities	Periodic
Weak	Occasional	Provides no real benefits	Rare
Transactional	Episodic	None to speak of	Very rare

Optimal relationships

Optimal relationships are with people who are much more likely to actively contribute to making you extremely successful. These powerful relationships can often translate into continuing achievements. These people are working hard to help you reach your intermediary goals that give you the ability to reach your end goals. Optimal business relationships foster success that breeds more success.

Your business reputation can make a very big difference in your fortunes and those of your company. Your professional brand, for instance, can make negotiations easier and prompt more people to work with (and for) you. Optimal relationships help you create a stockpile of stature and goodwill. In effect, you're able to considerably monetize a very powerful professional brand that extends beyond these people.

Optimal relationships often are active sources of new opportunities for you. The individuals in those relationships will be keenly aware of what you're interested in and energetically looking for people who can help you excel.

Strong relationships

If you have strong relationships, success is common but more intermittent. You end up with a great reputation, but it's not as good as it could possibly be. Also, now and again—not regularly—other people will bring you interesting and potentially fruitful opportunities.

Weak and transactional relationships

Your circumstances deteriorate somewhat when your business relationships are weak. In particular, transactional relationships are just a few steps up from being nonexistent.

You can't optimize them all

With all the considerable advantages of optimal relationships, why not optimize all your business relationships?

Answer: It's just not possible. Establishing and nurturing optimal business relationships requires real time and effort. Very often, you might not have enough interactions necessary to take a relationship to the optimal level.

Example: If you're negotiating the sale of your company, it's not realistic to think you can build optimal relationships with buyers. Still, you can do a lot to build stronger relationships, which can make the negotiations work out better for you.

Making the most of each relationship

As noted, the number of optimal business relationships you have will be limited due to the time and effort it takes to build such deep relationships. That said, you can take just about any business situation you're in and significantly enhance the relationships with your business associates by using the Everyone Wins Process. This is the case whether the other people are employees, business owners or government officials you're negotiating with, or people with whom you're networking. It doesn't matter where they are on the hierarchy at the moment; smart use of the Everyone Wins Process can further strengthen those relationships.

Important: The Everyone Wins Process for enhancing and optimizing relationships is designed for one-on-one interactions that are highly personalized and focused. It's not aimed at helping you enhance relationships among large groups of people or big crowds such as you might find at industry conferences, corporate events and the like. It's all about interacting with another person so you can decide whether he or she can make a significant difference to your success. If the answer is yes, then you can choose to build a level of rapport that motivates that person to help you get the results you want.

Just to be clear: We're not talking about deception and manipulation. Instead, the Everyone Wins Process is all about making sure your business associates excel as you excel.

Next, we'll address how enhancing and optimizing relationships empowers you to get what you want even as you seek to help others around you achieve their own objectives.

CHAPTER 3

Why You Win

Certainly when it comes to your professional and business dealings, you need to win. That's a requirement. You're in business to win, however you define winning. If part of your definition is to become seriously wealthy—and it probably is, as noted earlier—then amassing a sizable personal fortune is a key criterion of your success.

Make no mistake: The Everyone Wins Process for enhancing and optimizing business relationships and the mindset behind it are designed to help *you* win big.

But here's the thing. We see that among the most successful ultra-wealthy entrepreneurs, winning is not only about them winning—it's also about their business associates winning. It's about—wait for it—EVERYBODY winning.

So to fully understand the purpose and the power of the Everyone Wins Process, it's helpful to first see an important connection—the connection between your own success as an entrepreneur and the success of the people surrounding you. This is a connection that is built when you seek to enhance your relationships with those people—and maybe even optimize them.

It's once again time to ask yourself some important questions:

Are my employees raving fans of my company?

Am I consistently able to go into business negotiations and get everything I need in order to be successful, along with a lot of what I want?

Are the people I'm networking with actively looking to help me connect with other businesspeople who can make a difference to me and my company?

When you use the Everyone Wins Process to enhance and optimize business relationships, you're able to answer **yes** to each of these questions. You win—in a big way—now and in the future.

For example, we find that top ultra-wealthy entrepreneurs are extraordinarily adept at showing employees how their vision for the company is great for everyone—for each person—at the company. They look for win-win outcomes in negotiations because that enables them to come away with better results than they would have gotten otherwise.

And when networking with people, those ultra-wealthy entrepreneurs generating the best results intentionally and carefully build rapport that drives people to want to regularly help them (in both large and small ways) because those people are getting value from the relationship.

The Everyone Wins Process gets these outcomes, and it does so ethically.

Valued business outcomes

When you build and foster Everyone Wins relationships in business, you set the stage for everyone involved to come out winning. To see how, consider the impact of enhanced relationships from the vantage point of three critical components of entrepreneurship—leadership, negotiating and networking. (See **Exhibit 3.1**.)

Exhibit 3.1 Valued Business Outcomes When You Enhance Business Relationships	
Leadership	• When you combine this with vision and insight, you're able to build a substantial and hyperloyal following. • You're able to do a great job of motivating others within and outside your company to do their very, very best so your company can excel. • People will stick with you even when things turn bad. • Those in your optimal business relationships will just about "follow you into hell."
Negotiating	• You're able to get the best deal possible pretty much regularly, recognizing that there are likely to be other deals to be made in the future. • You're building a reputation as someone who is fair and responsible, which makes more people want to do deals with you, thereby providing you many more opportunities. • To get consistently solid negotiating results, you need incredible leverage, strong relationships or both—and it's often so much easier and more certain to consistently enhance and possibly optimize relationships with the other side in order to get amazing outcomes. • Optimal business relationships with people on the other side are rare, but they sometimes happen for you, and you're able to get spectacular results.
Networking	• Other people are actively identifying resources and making robust introductions. • The introductions are closely aligned with people who have a good chance of being able to provide you with what you need and want. • Those in your business relationships understand what would help you and will be looking out for the right people to introduce to you—and when they find someone, they'll do everything in their power to make the connection work for you. • People in your optimal business relationships will become your fiercest advocates, intensely looking for and finding the people and making the introductions you need in order to supercharge your business.

Leadership

The very nature of leadership is that people are following you and working hard to make your company successful. They believe in your vision—for the business, for yourself and for them. The critical characteristic of a leader is the ability to garner loyalty and even create a powerful supportive culture. By enhancing or optimizing your relationships with your employees and showing them how following you will get them to *their* goals, you help build loyalty so everyone wins.

Negotiating

Here, we're talking about highly touted win-win outcomes where you get what you need (and some of what you want) and the other side also achieves significant aspects of their agenda.

When you help counterparties clearly see the value you bring to them in negotiations, you dramatically increase the probability that they will give you what you require and desire in a deal. All in all, you're much more likely to get the outcomes you're striving for. Likewise, the counterparties are going to be happy with how things turn out for them.

Important: Truly optimal business relationships are rare in negotiations. When they do happen, it's usually because you're repeatedly negotiating with the same people. Still, even in the most contentious negotiations, it's possible to enhance the relationships in ways that produce superior outcomes for both sides.

Networking

In networking, enhancing your relationships results in people becoming your motivated advocates. They make concerted efforts not just to work with you but also to find other people to work with you who can help you excel.

When this happen, you become "top of mind" with your advocates. When new possibilities arise, these people do all they can to connect you to them. Meanwhile, you end up doing the same for your business associates through your networking connections—which in turn creates even more motivation for those in your relationships to connect you to the best people. Think of it as a virtuous circle.

A bonus benefit

Your aim is to develop powerful working alliances with other people who can help you build an astounding company—one that enables you to become seriously wealthy, if that's one of your goals.

But there's so much more to your life than just business or money.

When you enhance and optimize business relationships, you're also setting the stage for life-enhancing possibilities. Those with whom you have strong and optimal business relationships are not only going to help you grow your company; they'll also be resources you can rely on when your personal life gets tough or when you need something for yourself or your family.

It's all about being able to call on people for favors—something that's more easily done when you're dealing with relationships that are part of the top sections of the hierarchy. Maybe it's getting preferential access to a specialty physician, helping your kid land a great job or even getting introduced to a celebrity. Regardless, when you help everyone win, you build a network of people who can greatly improve your life and the lives of people you care about most.

You build a great business and become seriously wealthy, and it's life-enhancing

When people believe in your vision for your company, it benefits them. It also benefits you by turning employees into loyal followers. When people see how you're helping them, they can become dedicated advocates looking to introduce you to the best opportunities around. Also, when you're doing deals, those on the other side actually want you to succeed. All of this is not only possible but also highly likely to occur with the Everyone Wins Process for enhancing and optimizing business relationships.

Note: Helping others win even as you win is not about charity or altruism. It's about how you can do business together, become very successful and help spread success all around. From a societal vantage point, it makes a big difference. We recognize that relatively few people are enhancing and optimizing business or personal relationships the way we're advocating. Those who do, however, are being rewarded professionally and personally—all while making a difference in the lives of many people around them. They are heroes.

Next, we turn our attention to the important role that other people will play in your getting what you most want and need. The fact is, to maximize your results, it's necessary to focus a great deal of your attention and effort on other people and make it all about them.

CHAPTER 4

It's All About Them

Let's be honest: Most of us are very self-focused. We care greatly about our goals and our needs. That doesn't mean we're not charitable or kind or caring toward others. However, too many entrepreneurs put their needs front and center without looking much beyond that.

This attitude and approach to entrepreneurship can severely limit your success. As a business owner, you need other people to help you achieve your agenda. Some of these people might work for you. Others are people you make deals with, such as vendors and suppliers. Still others may be in additional business relationships that can help you reach greater heights.

Regardless of who they are, you need them on your side and doing their best to help you. No one—not even the most driven and intelligent entrepreneurs in the world—builds an exceptional business or serious wealth alone. That means the needs, concerns and issues of others should be on your radar screen.

Consider some of the people you deal with who you think are likely very important to your future success. Now ask yourself these questions:

How well do I really know them?

What are their wishes and dreams for their business ventures or their career and for themselves and their loved ones?

What major concerns and anxieties plague them?

If you don't know or aren't certain of the answers, it's probably time to shift your focus and understand these crucial and potential allies better.

The fact is, the best way to get what *you* want and need is often to make a negotiation or other business situation all about *them*—the people "sitting across the table" from you.

Eliminating "should"

A smart way to begin to shift your focus is to stop saying and thinking in terms of the idea of what others "should" do.

That's the advice we repeatedly hear from many of the most successful ultra-wealthy entrepreneurs. Just because you believe someone should do something or should act a certain way, that doesn't mean they're going to do anything you believe they should.

Take stock of the many people you've dealt with as a business owner. How many of them did what you think they should have done in the way you think they should have done it? How effective have you been in getting your relationship partners to do what you think they should do?

We're confident that a good number of you have prepared for negotiations by thinking through what you feel the other side should say and do—only to find that the other party ended up surprising you by not following the pre-scripted scenario you concocted in your head.

The bottom line is that when it comes to getting other people to behave in ways that can benefit you (as well as themselves), what you think they should or shouldn't do *doesn't matter*. This is usually the case in most aspects of life, and it becomes especially true when you're looking to enhance or optimize business relationships.

Focusing on what you think other people should do for or with you is essentially no different from talking to a recalcitrant teenager, a headstrong toddler or a badly overprivileged spouse. No matter the infallible logic of your argument—no matter the "obviousness" of your point of view—they are going to act as *they think* they should act. Your opinion has little to no value.

That means you risk a lot by focusing on what you think other people should or shouldn't do. For example, you'll likely become frustrated and maybe even angry when those people fail to live up to your expectations. In negotiation situations—especially high-stakes ones—frustration and anger can easily make the situation worse for you and prevent you from achieving your ideal outcomes.

Enlightened self-interest: aligning your interests with others' interests

The good news: There is a way to make it much more likely that people you're dealing with will not only do what you think they should do but also take steps that will enable both you and them to come out as winners.

It's called *enlightened self-interest.*

Think of enlightened self-interest like this: If you can clearly show other people—employees, suppliers, potential partners and so on—how they will get the results *they* most want by helping you get the results *you* most want, you will very likely be able to enlist their support and resources to further your endeavors. You make the conversation about them—their self-interests, their goals, their needs and their concerns.

The outcome is that they'll help you not because they should but rather because you've made it crystal clear to them that your respective fortunes can be tied together—that they can achieve their key goals by working to further your pursuit of your key goals, and vice versa.

In showing that connecting your success and their success, you transform your respective self-interests into enlightened self-interests—objectives that are most likely to be achieved by working together.

Delivering value

If you can find a way to align *your* self-interests with *their* self-interests, it's highly likely you will get support for your actions and wishes. Or if you can find other ways to deliver value to those in your business relationships that can help them achieve their goals, they'll be strongly inclined to help you succeed.

Again, it's not because they should help you. They will help you because you are very explicitly helping them achieve their goals.

If you can't do either of these two things, you probably won't get their support. Always remember: People in your business relationships will enthusiastically work for your benefit when they see there's something important they will gain by doing so.

Helping "the other person"

The power of the Everyone Wins Process results largely from the fact that not many people understand or use it. Because relatively few people are adept at enhancing business relationships and seeking to have everyone come out as winners, you will gain an astounding competitive advantage if you master those skills.

The upshot: By making sure your efforts seek to help others, you maximize your own chances of achieving tremendous results in business and in life.

Those efforts may involve you identifying areas of enlightened self-interest between you and your business associates—and communicating them to those people so they can see the benefits of working with you. But your efforts can also be centered on adding value to the other people's businesses and lives in ways that motivate those people to return the favor and bring great value to your company or your life.

In either case, you can see the importance of making it all about them—not all about you—in your discussions, interactions and negotiations. Of course, your goals are paramount, but your approach to achieving those goals involves a deep focus on those around you rather than on just yourself.

In coaching entrepreneurs on creating significant personal fortunes, one of the biggest obstacles is getting them to shift their thinking from "me" to "them." For many entrepreneurs, it takes a little while to truly understand the considerable advantages gained by helping others achieve their goals.

Indeed, the concept of "giving to get" is a powerful driver of the actions we see top ultra-wealthy entrepreneurs take on a regular basis in order to win. We turn to this concept next.

CHAPTER 5

Give to Get

Without question, every person has his or her own goals and agendas and is looking out for his or her own welfare. We all focus on our own self-interests so we can pursue winning results as we define them.

Your ability to assist other people in achieving their goals and agendas can strongly motivate them to help you reach your goals and agendas, as noted in the last chapter. This is key to effective one-on-one leadership, skillful negotiations and the highest quality of networking.

Ask yourself these questions:

What am I doing to determine other people's self-interests and how those interests potentially connect to my own self-interests?

Am I aligning my self-interests with their self-interests?

Am I adding value to help them achieve their self-interests?

To enhance and optimize business relationships, you need to figure out what the people in those relationships desire and require, along with what makes them feel insecure and anxious. Armed with that information, you can position yourself as the perfect vehicle to deliver on those dreams and necessities while also helping mitigate the negatives.

The core idea behind the Everyone Wins Process is understanding and leveraging the self-interests of the people you do business with so you can motivate them to help you by using enlightened self-interest or adding value. Because your recommendations and actions benefit them, they are highly likely to say yes when you ask them for something.

Think of it as giving to get.

Two ways to give to get

There are two approaches you can use—direct alignment (i.e., enlightened self-interest) and delivering added value (see **Exhibit 5.1**). Both are commonly used by the most successful subset of ultra-wealthy entrepreneurs, who seek to help everyone win by either aligning their interests with the interests of others or providing significant value to others.

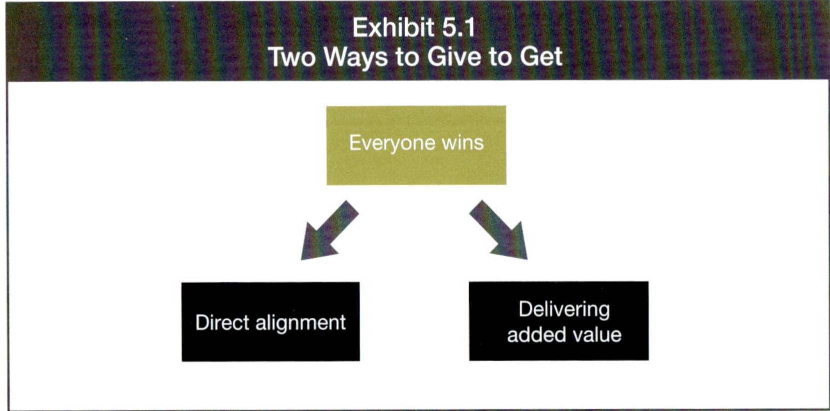

1. Direct alignment

One obvious example of direct alignment is when employees are compensated based in part on the profits of the company. Another is when a negotiation results in those on each side getting just what they want.

Direct alignment is when you and others have the same or very similar goals but usually for different reasons. Because everyone is aligned with the objective, the issue becomes *how* the different parties can get it.

As the owner of a company, you want your profits to soar to provide you with income and create equity value. If you can convey to your employees why this is good for them—how they can expect to benefit if the company's profits soar—then you have directly aligned your interests and created enlightened self-interest.

Connecting the dots for people makes it fairly easy for everyone to be in direct alignment. In the right circumstances, direct alignment is a pretty straightforward way to help everyone achieve their self-interests (**Exhibit 5.2**). That said, there may be times when some cleverness and mental effort are needed to identify meaningful overlap between self-interests.

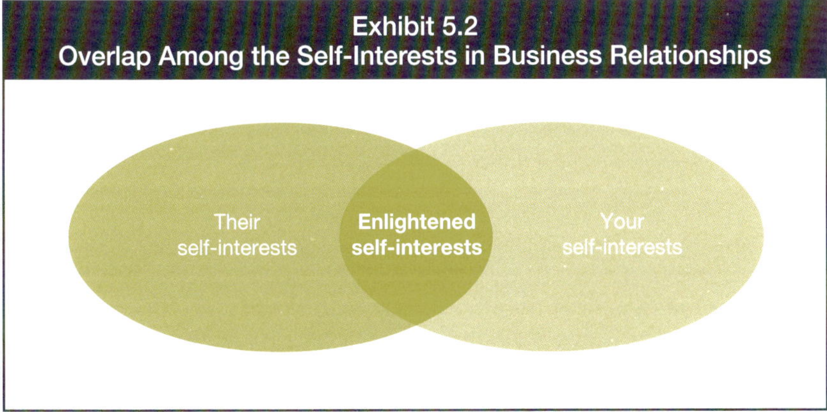

Caveat: The self-interests of those in your business relationships over time are likely to be different from yours. There are different objectives and agendas being pursued, so direct overlap will not always exist or easily be manufactured through effort.

2. Delivering added value

This approach is useful when you want something from those in your business relationships, but they want something different from you—in other words, when your interests are not aligned. In these situations, enlightened self-interest is not a possibility.

For example, you might want to be introduced to a prospective client whom a business associate knows. While that introduction might be obviously beneficial to you, there may be no obvious benefit to your associate in connecting the two of you. That means the person has to see why helping you can be advantageous for him or her.

Delivering added value operates as a sort of quid pro quo. You take certain actions to help those in your business relationships explicitly achieve their self-interests that are distinct from your own self-interests. Because you're helping them achieve their goals and agendas, they "owe" you. In order to pay you back, they'll be strongly inclined to fulfill your requests, take your recommendations and so on.

Simply put, when you help others get the results they want, they often become "indebted" to you. This can then motivate them to be helpful to you in achieving your goals. A little bit of diplomacy can go a long way.

Keep in mind, however, that this value-add approach doesn't typically result in a one-for-one arrangement, where you do something for someone in a business relationship and then that person immediately turns around and repays you. It's better to think about delivering added value as a gestalt; it's the composite of the value you bring over time (remember, you're playing the long game) that gets you significant help in return. As people's self-interests are almost always multifaceted, you should be looking to find different ways to be seriously helpful over the course of the relationship.

A competitive advantage

It would be very nice if everyone understood and adhered to the Everyone Wins Process. In our opinions, everyone in business—and probably in life—*should* (there's that word again) make every effort to enhance and optimize their relationships. It would make for a much more productive and supportive world. But of course, what we think *should* happen is, in many regards, meaningless.

Only a very select group of people uses the Everyone Wins Process to strategically and systematically enhance and optimize their business relationships. However, they're the ones who are most successful—certain ultra-wealthy, Super Rich and billionaire entrepreneurs. This highly successful group regularly tells us that one big reason for their competitive advantage is that they enhance and optimize relationships, while others do not.

Interestingly, when entrepreneurs start to see the power of the Everyone Wins Process, they often cannot understand why they didn't take this approach before (and why other business owners are not doing so). In personal wealth creation coaching, entrepreneurs regularly get substantial results very quickly—thereby proving to themselves the benefits of the approach.

The Everyone Wins Process is available to everyone. It's a powerful way to get what you want by helping other people get what they want due to the direct and very potent link between those two outcomes.

As noted, delivering added value is a common way that top ultra-wealthy entrepreneurs help others (and consequently themselves) reach their goals. The reason this works is due to the Law of Reciprocity—to which we now turn our attention.

CHAPTER 6

Leverage the Law of Reciprocity

By acting to further others' agendas and help them meet their goals, you will ultimately be able to meet your own goals. When you help those in your business relationships get the results they want, they often become indebted to you. This can then motivate them to be helpful to you—which can be hugely beneficial to you getting what you want in business (and in life). It's all about delivering added value.

Ask yourself these questions:

When someone does me a favor, do I naturally feel I owe that person something in return and seek to return the favor?

When I offer advice and people take it, do they tend to be indebted to me?

Do I keep track of the favors I give, expecting favors in return?

If you responded yes to any of the questions, you are implicitly following something called the Law of Reciprocity.

We're all familiar with the cause-and effect relationship of getting what you give—that what you "put out there" is what ultimately comes back to you. The most successful ultra-wealthy entrepreneurs understand this dynamic very well and regularly use it to put themselves on the receiving end of support and favors from the people they help. They habitually use it to build their businesses and their personal wealth and improve their situations in a myriad of ways.

In most instances, the Law of Reciprocity is why the Everyone Wins Process works so well.

If you want to truly harness the power of the Everyone Wins Process and get the results you desire consistently over time, you need to adopt the type of reciprocity mindset we see among the select group of ultra-wealthy entrepreneurs who are generating the highest levels of success.

Here's how you can do exactly that.

Get to yes

When someone does you a favor, you naturally feel you owe that person something in return and seek to return the favor—you're obligated to respond in kind. Likewise, when you do something valuable for others, they will feel they owe you and make efforts to "balance the scale."

This is known as the Law of Reciprocity.

Of course, it's more a guideline than a formal law. It's very likely that people you help will help you back—but there's no guarantee. There are even some people for whom the Law of Reciprocity rarely if ever applies. We categorize them as difficult and sometimes even as monsters (more on them later, in **Part III: When It Gets Harder**).

Still, reciprocity is pervasive throughout human culture. One reason is because it fosters interconnectedness; it's instrumental to social evolution. People are able to "give away" resources without having to just give them away, promoting sharing and the division of labor. The Law of Reciprocity is in evidence throughout society. For example:

- Free samples at department stores are intended to introduce people to a product and motivate these same people to buy the product in response to the gift.

- People often donate to politicians because they believe they can approach those politicians down the line to voice their concerns and be heard.

- Businesspeople do favors for each other and expect favors in return.

The societal benefits of the Law of Reciprocity are powerful enough that most people develop a sense of obligation to others for their beneficial actions. Consequently, we may feel internal pressures (such as anxiety) and external pressures (such as shame) to give back. For example, people who fail to give back can be ostracized and labeled as freeloaders.

The upshot: The Law of Reciprocity is a powerful way to get those in your business relationships to say yes to you.

Even better, the Law of Reciprocity usually has a multiplier effect—that is, you may end up receiving much more than you give. By giving freely, you potentially get back many times more.

This is not about control, mind you. Nor is it about persuasion. It's about helping other people and their helping you so there is more for everyone.

The aim is to increase the probability of your getting the results you are looking for and helping others achieve their self-interests.

The Law of Reciprocity is an underlying psychological dynamic of the Everyone Wins Process. Leveraging the Law of Reciprocity is the most common way to enhance and optimize business relationships and build relationships that reach the optimal category in the business relationship hierarchy.

Lead the charge

The Law of Reciprocity not only results in a psychological obligation to repay constructive actions, but it also creates a psychological obligation to receive advice and favors. Unrequested help that generates good results can produce a sense of indebtedness. The best ultra-wealthy entrepreneurs tend to understand this and seek to help others even before they're asked—which also ends up helping them, of course.

Indeed, we find that top ultra-wealthy entrepreneurs regularly evaluate business situations with an eye to helping the people involved. If they have powerful potential solutions to an issue, they take it upon themselves to offer those solutions to others. When these solutions produce positive outcomes, those who benefited from their generosity will likely feel they owe them a favor.

Once again, there's no guarantee that voluntarily helping someone will get you a benefit down the road. Nevertheless, leading the charge with the Law of Reciprocity by delivering value can make it more likely that you get much-needed support at some point—support that will help you achieve your objectives.

Say it again: All business relationships can be enhanced

Remember from **Chapter 2: The Business Relationship Hierarchy** that not all your business relationships can possibly reach the optimal level of the hierarchy. But you can further enhance just about any business relationship you choose. When you do, you will increase the likelihood of achieving your goals and winning (as you define it).

Now that you understand some of the key concepts that underpin the Everyone Wins Process, it's time to dive into the action steps. Next up: how to put the process to work.

PART II

The Everyone Wins Process

Armed with the mindset and principles that form the foundation of the Everyone Wins Process, you're now ready to learn how to implement the key steps in the process.

As you will see, the starting point is you—you must get clear about your own goals, objectives and self-interests in order to know the target you're shooting for so you can identify ways to help others who can also benefit you.

From there, you'll focus on the needs, wants and concerns of the people in your business relationships. This step involves a series of tools and tactics for getting others to share information with you and for ensuring that you end up with accurate, important details that will inform your Everyone Wins Process efforts.

Next, you'll identify ways to get what you need and want by benefiting others, based on enlightened self-interests, the Law of Reciprocity or both. This is where the rubber meets the road and you generate big results.

Finally, you'll discover how to track and assess those results to determine the value you're bringing to your relationships and the value you're receiving from them so you can make informed decisions about how to proceed for maximum results going forward.

CHAPTER 7

The Everyone Wins Process: An Overview

We find that the most successful ultra-wealthy entrepreneurs are adept at strengthening and enhancing their business relationships in any situation. Their ability to do this repeatedly is instrumental to their significant business and personal financial success.

So let's consider how enhancing and optimizing your business relationships affects you. Ask yourself these questions:

Specifically, what advantages are there for me to enhance and optimize my business relationships?

By enhancing and optimizing my business relationships, how much easier would it be to achieve my business and personal financial goals?

How willing am I to take responsibility for becoming so much more successful?

The fact is, enhancing business relationships translates into much greater professional and personal success for nearly all entrepreneurs. We've seen (and helped) some entrepreneurs achieve 10 or more times their current level of success—often much more. The upside is simply fantastic.

But if you want the substantial benefits that come with stronger business relationships, it's up to you to make them happen. Never assume the other people around you are using—or are even aware of—the concepts we're outlining in this book. In fact, we know from researching and talking to ultra-wealthy business owners and less-affluent entrepreneurs that most people are not. Because so few entrepreneurs are enhancing or optimizing their business relationships or even trying to, you can give yourself a substantial competitive advantage by adopting the Everyone Wins Process.

To get there, the focus of your conversations and actions with those in your business relationships has to be on them. You need to accurately understand their self-interests so you can find alignment or deliver added value—all the while keeping your self-interest top of mind but in the background.

The four-step Everyone Wins Process

The Everyone Wins Process is essential in all forms of personal wealth coaching. It consists of four main steps as shown in **Exhibit 7.1**.

Following is a big-picture look at the process. We will explore each step in greater detail in the chapters to come.

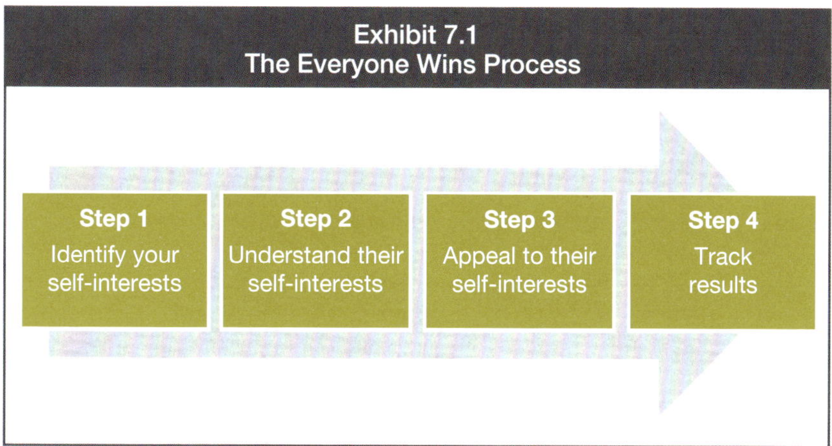

Step 1: Identify your self-interests

You must start by being very clear about your most important goals, issues and concerns. You need to know what winning means to you—what those outcomes look like in detail. Armed with that clarity, you can determine what you are looking for from your business relationships—which, in turn, will enable you to identify areas of direct alignment or ways to deliver value.

Step 2: Understand their self-interests

Identify what they want and need. Determining what's extremely important (as well as what is not important) to someone else can be challenging, especially when the other people aren't forthcoming. It's quite common for entrepreneurs and high-level executives to hide their goals and perspectives from "the other side."

Top ultra-wealthy entrepreneurs are generally adept at unearthing what is positively meaningful (e.g., aspirations) and negatively meaningful (e.g., fears) to the people they're dealing with. Typically, they accomplish this by employing three interconnected methodologies:

- **Tuning in.** You need to convey by your presence that you're interested and concerned. Listen—and look them in the eyes when you do. Be authentic.

- **Discovery.** You cannot give to get until you artfully use questions and probes to get insight into what really matters as well as what causes them concern.

- **Empathy.** Empathy is intertwined with discovery. You need to sincerely understand other people from their vantage point and know what it's like to "walk in their shoes." You also need to make sure they understand that you possess this deep insight about them.

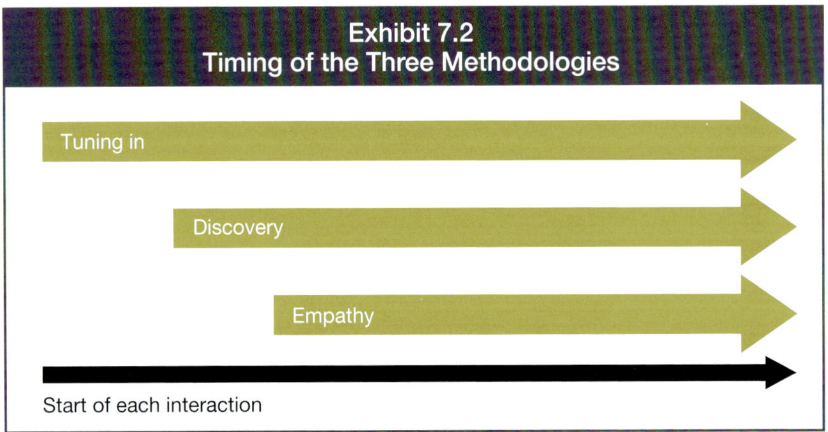

Once you start a conversation, you should use all three methodologies (see Exhibit 7.2). You will tune in and engage in discovery. As you collect information, you will employ empathy to determine whether you are interpreting the information correctly and to communicate to those involved that you understand them.

These three methodologies are so important to the Everyone Wins Process that we will devote a chapter to each going forward.

Step 3: Appeal to their self-interests

As we discussed in **Chapter 5: Give to Get**, there are two basic approaches you can take to help other people achieve their self-interests: direct alignment and added value.

With direct alignment, you concentrate on the overlap between your self-interests and the self-interests of those with whom you are dealing. The more overlap that exists and the more your respective actions further your shared goals, the easier it is to reach agreement and move forward to pursue mutual success by supporting each other. We refer to this as ensuring everybody's enlightened self-interests.

With delivering added value, you're using your capabilities, insights and connections to help other people achieve goals and agendas that differ from or are not directly connected to yours. This enables you to tap into the Law of Reciprocity, which drives those people you help to help you in return.

Note: Appealing to people's self-interests isn't about trying to persuade or convince them that an opportunity exists or that you can substantially help them achieve their agendas. It's about accentuating the opportunities for success that *actually do exist* in a situation. It's about making determined efforts to help other people accomplish their objectives and make their dreams real.

Step 4: Track results

When you track results, you can accelerate your success. Ultra-wealthy entrepreneurs are rarely interested in good intentions unless they're accompanied by good results. Good intentions without meaningful results are ultimately just nice thoughts—and nice thoughts don't create highly successful companies or build serious personal wealth.

As you use the Everyone Wins Process, the only way you will know if your actions have helped others achieve their self-interests is if you track results. Likewise, you need to track results to see if your efforts to help others have translated into their helping you attain better outcomes for you and your own business.

By tracking results—yours and those of people in your business relationships—you can determine where to best focus your efforts to maximize your future success. For example, you might decide to optimize other business relationships. You might choose to refine the added value you're providing. It all depends on how the situations are playing out—and, of course, you can't know how they're playing out if you're not paying attention.

Helping others achieve their dreams so they'll help you achieve yours

Ultimately, many people you deal with in business are going to be thinking mainly or exclusively about themselves. They're all about their goals and agendas, their fears and insecurities. By using the Everyone Wins Process and capitalizing on the concepts of enlightened self-interest and added value, you can change the entire game by creating significant business possibilities for *everyone.*

Help other businesspeople get what they seek and you'll find them taking actions that will make YOU a winner as you define it.

So for every person in every business situation with whom you want to enhance or optimize the relationship, ask yourself:

Do I really understand their self-interests?

If the answer is yes, then ask yourself:

Am I helping them achieve their self-interests so they will help me achieve my self-interests?

If not, ask yourself:

How can I help them achieve their self-interests?

Next, let's take deeper dives into each of the four main steps of the Everyone Wins Process so you make them work for you, your business and those in your business relationships.

CHAPTER 8

Get Clear on Your Self-Interests

To enhance and optimize your business relationships, you need to have a precise understanding of your own goals and interests going into any dealings with the people in those relationships. In other words, before you can help others in ways that enlist them to help you, you first have to know what you want to achieve and what concerns you have about those goals.

In short, your self-interests are the lens through which you view all your business dealings and all your business relationships. If you don't have a deep understanding of your own interests, you won't be able to identify and highlight the enlightened self-interests that you and others might share. And you won't be able to capitalize on the value you deliver to other people by getting what you most want in return.

Remember from **Chapter 1: What Is Winning?** that the most successful of the ultra-wealthy entrepreneurs, by and large, go to great lengths to home in on their self-interests. This clarity separates them from the majority of less-accomplished entrepreneurs—and even most of their ultra-wealthy peers.

So ask yourself these questions:

Am I very clear about what winning means to me?

Am I very clear about the intermediary goals I need to achieve in order to reach my end goals?

If so, do I bring this knowledge with me to every business situation?

Gaining clarity

Most entrepreneurs go into business meetings with an agenda. But they tend to think only about immediate or short-term outcomes rather than consider a wide range of possibilities. Very few regularly go into meetings with aims and a sense of purpose that come from being acutely aware of their own self-interests.

You need to do what the best ultra-wealthy entrepreneurs do: Approach each and every business situation looking for ways the people involved can help you in both the short and long terms.

As time is precious, always ask yourself: *How do I benefit—and how can I potentially benefit—by dealing with this person?*

You can go deeper by answering questions such as:

- What outcome of this meeting would satisfy me? If the outcome I'm looking for is not happening, what do I need to do to make things work better?

- Where is this person on the business relationship hierarchy (from **Chapter 2**)? Where would I prefer him or her to be, given my goals?

- What results with this person would make me feel I've been extremely successful? And what are my minimum acceptable results?

- What happens if we don't reach an understanding?

- What opportunities are there for me in the longer term by working with this person and enhancing our relationship? What will I need to do to take advantage of these opportunities?

Important: This doesn't mean you won't have meetings that are exploratory in nature. Sometimes you have getting-to-know-you meetings. Nevertheless, you want to determine (as fast as possible) the probability of a new business associate being helpful in achieving your self-interests, and act accordingly.

From select ultra-wealthy entrepreneurs, we understand that this way of thinking—considering the business relationship and the interaction from different perspectives—takes mental effort. You have to remain keenly aware of all your goals, including your intermediary and end goals, at all times. Consequently, as discussions go off in directions different from those you anticipated, you must never lose sight of what you need to accomplish. You might, for example, determine that a person should be someone with whom you have a strong relationship. But over time, you see that's not the way it's going to work out. So you change gears and seek to further enhance the relationship only in certain situations.

Success tip: Don't shortchange yourself. Great aspirations are more likely to foster great results. Failing to think bigger almost always guarantees you'll achieve less. Know what you really want, and go for it.

Once you have clarity and focus on you and your interests, it's time to do the same with those with whom you're doing business—which brings us to the next step in the Everybody Wins Process.

CHAPTER 9

Tune in to Identify Wants and Needs

After you're clear about your own self-interests, you must focus your attention on those interests of the people with whom you want enhanced or optimized business relationships. This step is so important that we are devoting the next three chapters to the strategies and tactics you'll need in order to gain a deep understanding of goals, needs, wants, concerns and other crucial issues of those in your business relationships.

Your first step is to tune in to them. When you tune in to someone, you're giving him or her your undivided attention. This is where enhancing business relationships starts. Being appropriately attentive sets the stage for building rapport that will reveal the other person's goals and concerns.

Most of us are sensitive, consciously and subconsciously, to the attention and inattention other people give us. We welcome expressions of concern, and we find being disregarded and discounted hurtful. During times of crisis—a relative being sick, a death in the family or another type of highly stressful situation—simply having someone there with us might make things easier.

Ask yourself these questions:

How does it feel when someone I am talking to is being very attentive?

How does it feel when someone I am talking to is focused on other things, such as a smartphone?

How often am I not fully engaged when dealing with other people in business?

When you tune in, you tell other people that you're there with them—what they're saying is important, and they matter. Most important, it lays the groundwork for you to develop a deep understanding of their self-interests so you can eventually identify areas of enlightened self-interests to emphasize in your dealings with them or to identify ways you can add value to their lives that will encourage them to reciprocate.

Tuning in is a function of your frame of mind, and you can see it in both verbal and nonverbal behaviors. We'll explore each.

Verbal behavior: the art of impactful listening

Tuning in requires you to focus on what another person is saying, of course. That means you need to become adept at *impactful listening*.

Listening is a skill that is easy to understand but tough to do well consistently. For most businesspeople, "listening" really is just waiting for their turn to talk. They're patiently biding their time until they can say something they consider insightful and worthwhile.

But learning to listen impactfully can really pay off. Why? Because it is an expression of authenticity. Also, the very act of listening has a positive bearing on outcomes, which helps you enhance your business relationships.

Most people, for example, usually love to talk about their businesses, their families and themselves. This gives you an opportunity to learn important information you can then use to develop a solid understanding of them and their agendas. Therefore, impactful listening is essential to discerning their self-interests.

Impactful listening is all about capturing and truly understanding the messages another person is communicating. It also entails understanding the context—the current situation, the backstory and the expectations of those in your business relationships.

Additionally, impactful listening is listening with an open mind in a noncritical manner that seeks to shut down the inherent biases we all have that can interfere with our ability to listen closely and interpret honestly. Such open-minded listening is necessary to enhance and optimize business relationships, especially when dealing with difficult people or those who don't share our worldview or values.

The most successful ultra-wealthy entrepreneurs tend to be excellent impactful listeners. They are highly engaged in and intensely curious about what other people are saying. Their listening is usually indicative of caring behavior. But let's not disregard the business advantages of impactful listening. It aids ultra-wealthy entrepreneurs in their leadership efforts, in negotiation success, in effective networking—and in becoming seriously wealthy.

The benefits of impactful listening are powerful. For example, impactful listening is a very potent means of intelligence-gathering that enables you to discern people's intentions, dreams, wishes and fears. Top ultra-wealthy entrepreneurs carefully and perceptively listen to the businesspeople they're dealing with so they can collect information and perspectives that will further empower them to find areas of commonality and deliver added value.

Just like these ultra-wealthy entrepreneurs, you want to listen to what other people are saying as well as how they are saying it. You're listening for:

- Central and defining messages
- The person's strengths and weaknesses
- Experiences, good and bad, that drive the person's thinking and behavior
- How and what someone thinks about certain matters
- How the person's feelings and emotions convert into actions
- Information someone isn't sharing or is only implying
- The person's latent and unexpressed needs

Impactful listening with this level of commitment and intensity is especially helpful when you lack experience dealing with a particular person, as it gives you an understanding of how the person thinks and reacts. This understanding in turn can help you know the person's self-interests and therefore predict his or her actions and decisions with more confidence.

Important: Impactful listening also involves tuning in to a person's *nonverbal* behavior. You need to "read" what other people are saying with their bodies, eye movements and so forth. Are they communicating interest, respect and caring—or the opposite?

You will usually be well served if you pay attention to how people:

- Maintain good eye contact
- Position themselves physically relative to you
- Smile, frown and use other facial expressions in response to what each of you says

Clearly, impactful listening takes effort—it just doesn't happen. Our default position is usually some type of bad listening—catching only parts of what someone says, hearing only what we want to hear and ignoring the rest, or thinking about what we want to say and ignoring what the other person is saying. To use the Everyone Wins Process effectively, bad listening habits have to be replaced by impactful listening skills.

Your nonverbal behaviors

Tuning in goes beyond your ability to listen impactfully to someone else. It also includes your own skills at demonstrating that you are focused on the person in front of you.

For example, if someone were to observe you interacting with other people, you would want them to clearly see *just by looking at you* that you are giving those people your full attention. When we watch highly successful ultra-wealthy entrepreneurs connecting with other people, it's evident that they're completely engaged.

Our faces and bodies can express a lot without our even saying a word. There are a number of nonverbal behaviors that tell other people you're paying attention and communicate that you are "there" and you care. You can use those behaviors to:

- Direct and focus the conversation
- Communicate feelings and sentiments
- Adjust, refine or add nuance to your verbal messages

Your nonverbal behavior is a very potent way of highlighting and augmenting what you say. Sarcasm, for example, can be communicated nonverbally. Nonverbal behaviors can sometimes be even more important than the words you use. For example, people you interact with for business will likely decide how interested in and committed to them you are based largely on your nonverbal signals. That in turn will directly impact their interest in and commitment to you and your success.

By being physically attentive and tuned in to others, you encourage them to trust you and share important details with you—details that will help you identify enlightened self-interests and opportunities to provide value.

The following are four of the nonverbal action steps we see the best ultra-wealthy entrepreneurs regularly take.

1. Maintain good eye contact

Fairly steady eye contact says to the other person, "I'm interested in you. I'm paying attention, and I want to know you and hear what you're saying."

Important: Good eye contact does **not** mean staring at or fixating on the person. Intense, unmitigated staring will often scare people away and may give them the impression there's something "off" about you. Good eye contact includes occasionally looking away—just not so often that the other person mistakenly thinks you're not interested.

2. Adopt an engaging posture

Your body orientation should say, "I'm here to learn about you and to be helpful to you." Keeping an open posture shows that you're open to what other people are saying. In contrast, crossing your arms and legs tends to convey that you're holding back or you're less available. Likewise, leaning toward someone conveys that you're concerned, interested and attentive. Leaning back or away suggests the opposite.

3. Relax

When you're relaxed, you appear more confident and capable to others than if you are obviously nervous or fidgety. That in turn makes it more likely that other people will be comfortable with you and therefore more willing to share.

You want to be very much at ease with the people around you, which will make them much more at ease with you. Anything that takes away from the perception that you're there with someone *in that moment* will subtract from the relationship.

4. Align your words with your expressions

When enhancing business relationships, you're going to regularly be strategic about what you say. Make sure your facial expressions aren't saying something different from what the words you're using do. You can be upbeat about an idea, for example, and become more animated—conveying excitement—as you describe the idea.

Nothing else happens if you don't tune in

Tuning in to others is a foundational step in the Everyone Wins Process. All the remaining steps flow from your ability to focus in a nonjudgmental and constructive way on the verbal and nonverbal messages someone else is sending.

Remember, a big part of the Everyone Wins Process is to make it all about the other person. Tuning in from the start will enable you to do exactly that—and make a powerful impression so others will open up and share key information you need to know in order to win.

That said, you need to extract the information—and we turn to the process of discovery next.

CHAPTER 10

Engage in Discovery to Identify Wants and Needs

The discovery step is where your ability to tune in truly pays off, as you artfully use questions and probes to get the required insight into what really matters to others—as well as what causes them concern.

You are going to tune in to other people once you engage. And when you do engage, you need to discover the answers to these questions:

What is and is not meaningful in their worlds?

What are their wishes and dreams, anxieties and concerns?

What are their self-interests?

Discovery is all about actively gathering information that you interpret in order to form usable insights. You want to understand both the big picture and the critical nuances from the perspective of those in your business relationships.

Curiosity is a must

Before you can effectively ask open-ended questioning and probe for information that will allow you to determine a person's self-interests, you have to adopt a curiosity mindset.

Curiosity connects to all aspects of human advancement. It's the fundamental psychological concept behind learning. It makes you a better leader, negotiator and networker.

Being curious means you're sincerely interested in the lives of other people in a very broad way. Being interested in a single aspect (or a small number of aspects) of someone else isn't curiosity.

Curiosity lets you move far beyond using checklists, decision trees or scripts. It enables you to immerse yourself in discovering what makes someone tick, which is central to enhancing and optimizing business relationships.

The self-interests framework

It's smart to organize your curiosity, and the questions it will inevitably generate, within a framework.

Indeed, it's very characteristic of the most successful ultra-wealthy entrepreneurs to have a questioning strategy for each business relationship in each situation. In the Everyone Wins Process, when it comes to your business relationships, you're looking for self-interests so you can identify areas of direct alignment or ways to provide added value. The self-interests framework (see **Exhibit 10.1**) is a way to think about getting that information.

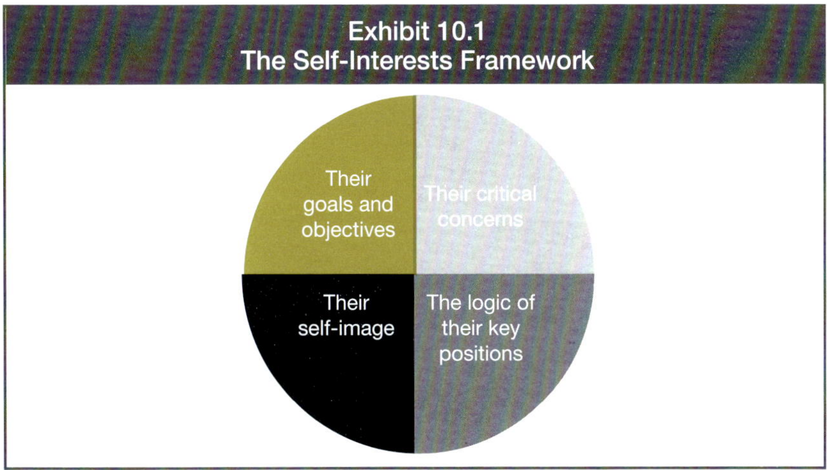

This framework includes these elements:

- **Their goals and objectives.** You need to know just what those with whom you are dealing want to accomplish—their end goals as well as their intermediate-term goals. Without this information, you can't see how your goals and their goals potentially align and interrelate—or how you will be able to add value and help them achieve their agendas, thereby motivating them to reciprocate.

- **Their critical concerns.** Always look for information that helps you understand what matters to them and where and why their time and energy are focused. Knowing what has their attention gives you insights into their actions—and possibly provides you with ways you can help them more quickly address their agendas.

- **Their self-image.** This is about how they want to see themselves as well as how they want others to see them. Businesspeople will rarely take actions that conflict with their self-image. This includes their perspective on their strengths and weaknesses as well as their anxieties and insecurities (you will have your own assessment of these traits as well).

- **The logic of their key positions with supporting evidence.** You want to know the basis of their thoughts and feelings, so identify the facts and perspectives they're relying on and the experiences that underpin their viewpoints and actions. This includes their unshakable beliefs.

The upshot: To enhance and optimize your business relationships, you have to know a lot about the people in those relationships. You want to know not only the facts but also how those people interpret the facts and how they feel about what the facts mean.

Pro tip: Do as many of the top ultra-wealthy entrepreneurs do—go into initial meetings with an attitude that you know nothing about the person you'll be dealing with. This can help you avoid making fallacious conjectures and keep your biases out of your assessment. In short, "ignorance" can serve you well. In fact, we refer to this as "professional ignorance."

Going beyond the framework

While the self-interests framework is useful for understanding the motivations and actions of those with whom you do business, you may sometimes need to learn even more about them to find alignment or deliver added value and to determine ways in which they can help you.

For example, say you're networking. The following are a couple of additional categories you might include in your discovery conversations:

- **The characteristics of their professional networks.** This includes whom they do business with and the strength of these relationships.

You want to see the extent of their networks and the obligations they are owed (or owe). This way, you can develop strategies that foster their sharing relationships that would be helpful to you.

- **The resources they can access.** You might seek to find out how are they presently using their networks, along with which capabilities in their networks they're not capitalizing on. By gaining this knowledge, you can ascertain the resources at their disposal that can be useful to them and to you.

Discovery approach #1: Using open-ended questions

When engaging in discovery, the obvious path is through direct questions. And why not? Asking questions is how you learn about other people. Your ability to go into meetings wanting to learn and asking smart questions is crucial to enhancing or optimizing your business relationships.

Asking relevant and intelligent questions not only gets you the insights you're looking for, but also projects to others that you have a high level of competence, credibility and capability; they believe that competent people ask smart questions. One ultra-wealthy entrepreneur explained to us that the more questions he asks and the less he talks, the smarter people think he is. It works this way for just about everyone.

The best way to elicit business associates' thoughts, feelings, intentions and concerns is to use open-ended questions—that is, questions that cannot be answered with simple short answers such as yes or no. Open-ended questions are designed to get expansive, meaningful answers from people by requiring them to think and elaborate. Such questions are good at building trust and rapport as well as generating lots of information.

Useful open-ended questioning often starts with words such as what, why and how. Some that have proven to be consistently useful can be found in **Exhibit 10.2**.

Exhibit 10.2 Some Useful Questions	
Question	**Purpose**
What can you tell me about your business (profession, yourself)?	This is what often matters most to people. After asking the question and letting them talk, you'll likely get a great deal of information.
What's the most important thing we should be discussing?	You want to make sure you are truly being responsive. At the same time, you want to move your agenda along.
What are you most concerned about?	Knowing what is very important to them provides insights into how you can determine possible areas of commonality or deliver added value, and it demonstrates that you are indeed focused on them.
What do you think?	This generates involvement and uncovers their perspectives. It's very useful to help you better understand their frames of reference.
What are the best and worst outcomes?	Knowing what people are hoping for and fearing in a particular situation can be instrumental in giving you direction on how to be helpful and supportive.

Caveat: When introduced to the Everyone Wins Process, many entrepreneurs look for specifics about what to ask and when. They'd like a script. Many of them would like to know what question to ask first, second, third and so forth. The problem is that other people will not have read the script. That's why it's better to stay flexible with your questions and to focus more on the categories in the self-interests framework rather than on specific questions in a specific order. This approach will give you more versatility and power to adapt "on the fly" based on what you're hearing from a particular person.

When we coach entrepreneurs on building a substantial personal fortune, many of them initially have some trouble knowing what questions to ask and when to ask them. Using the self-interests framework coupled with sincere curiosity, they pretty quickly become proficient at using open-ended questions and knowing how best to follow up.

Tempering open-ended questions

Sometimes people react negatively to certain questions. Whenever you're unsure and think there might be blowback if you were to ask a particular question, it's wise to *temper* it.

There are different ways to do so. One very effective approach is to use disclaimers, which can take the "sting" out of open-ended questions and give you some cover if you're met with resistance. Examples of disclaimers include:

- "I'm not sure how to ask this, but …"
- "Without imposing, may I ask you about …"
- "I don't want to make you uncomfortable, but …"
- "If I'm being too forward let me know, but …"
- "This might be touchy, but may I ask you about …"

If you want to ask someone about his or her income and you think it might turn that person off, you can say, "I'm not sure how to ask this, but are you earning enough to support your lifestyle?" If the question is offensive, the person will often say something along the lines of "Let's not talk about that." So you move on to something else—quickly. On the other hand, you might very well get the information you seek.

It's important to keep the conversation moving forward. If people are reticent about some matters, tempering open-ended questions usually makes it easy for them to not answer without closing down or further limiting the conversation.

Success tip: By being curious, you naturally will find that it's easy to use open-ended questions to give you the depth of understanding you'll need in order to enhance and optimize your business relationships. That said, practicing constructing and using open-ended questions is usually essential to making discovery go smoothly.

From declarative statements to open-ended questions

Forming and asking smart open-ended questions, and doing so repeatedly, can be challenging. Frankly, when people are sure of themselves and their points of view, they are generally inclined to tell others what they think—but not to find out what others believe. They rely on statements, not questions.

Perhaps even you are guilty of this behavior. It's quite common for confident, hard-driving businesspeople to make extensive use of declarative statements. They're used to expressing opinions, beliefs, mantras and instructions.

The trouble is that declarative statements and extreme confidence do little for building rapport and collecting information—which you've got to do to enhance and optimize your relationships.

Based on our research, we find most entrepreneurs are more inclined to express their opinions and positions than to ask questions. They'll make proclamations when open-ended questions would serve their aims better.

Therefore, your goal must be to gather intelligence and move the process along by replacing declarative statements with open-ended questions.

Often, the dexterous and nimble use of open-ended questions can be the most efficacious way to not only gather critical intelligence but also further strengthen business relationships.

There are various ways to transform declarative statements into open-ended questions, including some very easy but highly effective formulaic methods.

1. Turn the declarative statement into a *question*.

> Declarative statement: *It's a difficult project.*
>
> Question: *Why is it a difficult project?*

2. Add the involvement of your business relationship.

> Declarative statement: *I don't see how your idea would work.*
>
> Question: *Why don't you tell me how your idea would work, considering the complications?*

3. Tag an open-ended question onto the declarative statement. (This is perhaps the easiest technique.)

> Declarative statement: *I'm going to change the company structure.*
>
> Question: *I'm going to change the company structure. How would you suggest I do so?*

One of the biggest benefits of using open-ended questions instead of declarative statements is that questions bring others more intensely into the conversation. By increasing their level of involvement and engagement, you're likely to exponentially enhance your connection with them. As a result, people will share more—giving you more power to enhance and optimize these business relationships and pursue your self-interests.

Discovery approach #2: Probing

Open-ended questions essentially get the ball rolling and allow you to start collecting a broad range of information. As that process unfolds, you will hear comments from the other person about which you would like to learn more—maybe much more. He or she will make some comments you believe are quite meaningful and may be useful in getting everyone to win. So you need to dig deeper.

When this happens, it's time to probe. Probing is all about focusing on a single issue or a handful of issues and digging deeper so you capture all the relevant details you need.

Probes are verbal and nonverbal forms of encouragement that signal you're very interested in what others said and you'd like them to share more.

Nonverbal encouragements include simple actions such as leaning in a little more toward the speaker and nodding your head in agreement. Verbal encouragements include comments such as "*Uh-huh,*" "*Yes,*" and "*Go on,*" which indicate you'd like the person to continue talking.

Verbal probing can also involve open-ended questions similar to those you asked initially—but it's adapted to extract more information and details. You can be looking for specific details, or you can want the other person to tell the story as he or she likes. Probably the most effective question (including variations) to use as a probe is this one:

Can you tell me more?

There are lots of ways to phrase probes. It often depends on the situation. Some more examples include:

- "How did that work for you?"
- "What did you learn for that experience?"
- "What more can you share?"

When you're probing, you're directly and simply asking for more information. By prompting people to go deeper, your knowledge of their worldview and their circumstances increases. The result is superior understanding that can readily translate into more commonalities and superior added value.

Selective repetition also often works well as a probe. When you want more information, just repeat key words or phrases the other person used. Here's an example:

> Other person: *After the meeting, we talked about getting a raise and taking over the division.*
>
> You: *After the meeting, you talked about it.*
>
> Other person: *Yes. He went into the details of what I would get and what I'd be responsible for.*

Probes are used to fill in missing information you think might be useful in order to enhance and optimize the relationship. It's often smart to follow certain open-ended questions and probes with empathetic responses.

Important: Discovery questions and empathetic responses should be smoothly interspersed in your conversations—that is, they're interconnected.

The 10 percent rule of discovery

Discovery is about learning the thoughts, ideas, beliefs and so forth of your business associates. Frankly, it's very hard to do that when you're talking. We're not suggesting you don't have important things to contribute to the conversation, but if you're talking a lot, you're likely not learning very much about the other person.

Important: The more you listen, the smarter you sound.

Our advice: Follow the 10 percent rule of discovery, which means you should not talk more than 10 percent of the time during a conversation if your intent is to ascertain the other person's self-interest. Talk more than that and you're probably not going to get him or her to open up and share what you need to know. As one ultra-wealthy entrepreneur explained to us, "You get to learn more when you can keep your mouth shut."

Indeed, we find that the less you talk, the smarter you probably appear. This has nothing to do with saying "stupid things" if you were to speak. It may sound strange, but generally, people tend to attribute greater intelligence and wisdom to people who ask questions and listen well.

You want to make every effort to have other people share themselves with you. The more they share, the easier it likely will be for you to enhance and optimize the business relationship. At this stage, by letting them do most of the talking, you're getting the information you need. Also, they're likely to be more receptive to your ideas and suggestions because they perceive you as caring and smart.

But there's another step here that you must take—it involves the use of empathy and empathetic listening skills to confirm you really understand the other person and to identify information that will be truly useful in helping you win. We turn to empathy next.

CHAPTER 11

Use Empathy to Identify Wants and Needs

Done well, the discovery process will give you a lot of information. Some of it obviously will be useful. Some of it may possibly be important. And some of it will be superfluous.

That means you're going to have to sift through all the information to confirm it and separate the diamonds from the coal. And that means you need to go beyond simply discovering information.

Ask yourself these questions:

Have I ever misinterpreted what someone has said to me?

Have I ever turned someone off because he or she thought I didn't understand?

Have I ever had a business relationship derail because of confusion over intent?

If you've answered yes to any these questions, congratulations—you're like almost everyone else. Human relationships are complex, and it's all too easy to misinterpret people's statements and the values and intentions that support them.

The good news: You can mitigate or even avoid these possible errors by being *empathetic.*

The empathy-accuracy connection

When you use empathetic statements and responses in your business dealings, you are able to determine whether you accurately have heard and interpreted information from others. Think of your empathetic responses as trial balloons. They're ways of confirming whether you're on the right track. Empathy helps reduce errors and misperceptions in business relationships.

Additionally, empathetic responses tell people you not only understand but also care—which in turn further motivates them to open up to you and reveal even more information that may help you identify their self-interests.

No one is perfect

Just as curiosity is central to discovery, caring is central to empathetic responses. By being empathetic, you're demonstrating respect for and an appreciation of others. This doesn't mean you necessarily agree with them. Empathy is not about agreeing; it's about understanding where others are coming from.

For example, you might find some of the values of a business associate abhorrent. Being empathetic means you recognize their values, the genesis of those values and how they motivate the person. But you'll probably always find those values abhorrent.

To become empathetic, it's helpful look in the mirror. Let's be honest: You have your own faults and failings, and everyone is dysfunctional to some degree. Hopefully you're accepting of and comfortable with yourself, and whatever dysfunctions you have don't badly impact your life and happiness.

By accepting your own issues and possible neuroses, you may find it easier to accept the dysfunctions in your business relationships. No one is perfect—far from it.

Being empathetic means you're able to get inside the frames of reference of others to and understand what they're thinking and feeling, and why. It's also your ability to communicate this understanding to them without prejudice.

The formula for empathetic responding

Empathetic responding takes a number of forms. The easiest way to be empathetic is to use this formula:

What + why = empathy

What describes what is going on; why is the explanation for what is going on. For example, you might respond to a business associate's statements in this way:

You feel (emotion) **because** (experience, thoughts behaviors).

Here are examples:

"**You feel** anxious **because** your partner is not seeing the big picture."

"**You're** angry **because** the buyer is trying to pull a fast one."

"**You're** disappointed **because** you thought you were going to meet the person in charge instead of a subordinate."

You can replace "feel" with other words—"want," "need," "believe," "expect" and so forth.

"**You want** to redo the agreement **because** there are more opportunities out there and you don't want to be handcuffed."

"**You expected** to get a chance to help negotiate the deal **because** you're the one who brought the other company to the table."

You can clearly see how such responses can help confirm whether you have heard and processed the other person's statements and information accurately. The person will respond with a yes or no to your empathetic statement—and will probably volunteer additional details either way.

Summarizing

Another very powerful way to respond empathetically is with summaries. Summarizing is articulating the essence of what the other person is saying and where you go from here. It's not a regurgitation but rather a distillation of what matters and what actions to take.

Summaries highlight key points, ideas and perspectives. You also can incorporate how the other person is making progress toward achieving his or her goals. The overarching goal, of course, is to lock in understanding.

Watching extremely successful ultra-wealthy entrepreneurs summarize parts or entire conversations is like watching a great magician do a trick that amazes you even though you know how the trick is done. Summaries can be very powerful at building rapport as well as providing focus and direction. Some ways to start summarizing include these:

- "To put all this in perspectives, you believe …"
- "Based on what we've discussed, …"
- "If I understand you correctly, …"

Keep in mind these two best practices when it comes to summarizing conversations:

1. **Use summaries at the right time.** Summaries can fit almost anywhere in a conversation to ensure you understand, to make sure the other person knows that you understand, to lock in agreements and to direct the conversation. Although summarizing may be used throughout the conversation, you'll certainly want to use it at the end. That way, you can delineate next steps and get commitment (see **Chapter 12: Appeal to the Self-Interests of Others**).

2. **Encourage the other person to do the summarizing.** It can be very helpful to have your business associate summarize the meeting. This usually results in him or her being more psychologically invested in working together toward your self-interests. It also gives you clues to what the other person found to be the most important moments of your interaction. To make this happen, you might use prompts such as these:

   - "What have we decided today?"
   - "Where are we?"
   - "What do we need to do next?"

Guidelines when responding empathetically

To increase accuracy and make sure you're keeping the conversation going smoothly and productively, the following empathetic response guidelines can prove useful:

- **Always think before responding.** It's usually a mistake to jump in too quickly. Reflect on what you heard, making clear you believe you know what it means. How does it relate to what you already know? How does it relate to the other person's perspectives and your self-interests?

- **Avoid interrupting to make a point.** Most people dislike being interrupted. Don't respond until you've determined the other person is finished talking. You can always ask whether he or she is completely finished before addressing any concerns.

- **Avoid pontificating.** Remember, it's all about the other person, whom you want to do most of the talking. As much as possible, keep your responses short, and be as pithy as you can.

- **Avoid being judgmental.** A person who feels judged is unlikely to open up and share important information with you—or to want to work with you. Try to see the person's situation from his or her perspective. Again, it's not about agreeing; it's about understanding.

- **Confirm the aspects of the other person's self-images you believe in.** You want to sincerely understand how others see themselves—be it kind, attractive, creative, self-reliant and so forth. And you want to make sure the person knows you recognize and appreciate those positive qualities. This tends to strengthen your relationship.

- **Avoid simply parroting what someone said.** Simply repeating what you heard is not being empathetic. It doesn't mean much when you are no better than a recorder. You need to be able to show empathy using your own words and interpretations.

- **Respond strategically.** It's impossible to respond empathetically to everything someone says. Therefore, as you're listening, you need to concentrate on the most important messages. You need to strategically choose what you will respond to. Look for what's central and most relevant in the particular situation.

Validating your understanding

Empathetic responses such as the what/why formula and the use of summaries can serve as your perception reality checks. Do you really understand what people are saying to you? Do you truly understand why they think as they do?

Empathy will give you answers to those and similar questions. If you discover that your interpretations are inaccurate, you can continue to probe and respond empathetically until you arrive at a crystal clear understanding of the other person—and his or her self-interests.

Next up: It's time to get results for them and for you.

CHAPTER 12

Appeal to the Self-Interests of Others

It's time to turn your in-depth understanding of your business associates into action.

You know your own self-interests thoroughly. You understand on a deep level the self-interests of specific business associates. Now you want to identify specific steps that you and they can take that will help both of you achieve those respective self-interests.

This is where enlightened self-interests come into play—showing others how helping you will enable them to reach their goals. When there are no direct areas of alignment to create enlightened self-interests, your approach will be to deliver added value to help those on the other side achieve their objectives—thereby triggering the Law of Reciprocity. Of course, there will be situations in which both approaches make sense and can be leveraged for maximum impact.

To appeal to the self-interests of others, ask yourself these questions:

Do I really understand the self-interests of the people with whom I am dealing?

Have I found meaningful and viable ways to help them achieve their interests?

Do I see a connection between my getting what I want and their getting what they want?

Am I confident about how I am going to communicate with them?

You need to be able to answer yes in order to strengthen and optimize these business relationships.

After determining where your goals are aligned or the ways you can deliver added value, your job is to get them on board with your agenda.

In fostering alignment or delivering added value, you continually must emphasize how anything you propose—any recommendation—will help them achieve their goals. By taking this tack, your conversations will be predominantly about them—not you.

You know what you want to gain—your self-interests. So you want to make the discussion all about their goals and objectives—their self-interests. Only after they see you as meaningfully supporting their agenda or helping them surmount their concerns can you most effectively introduce the ways they can help you.

Strategizing your efforts

Let's remind ourselves of what self-interests mean to you as an entrepreneur:

Individuals are motivated by what is most important to them—their most important goals and objectives. You want people to behave in ways that are supportive of your business endeavors, but they will do so not because they should but because you have shown them how it is in their best interests to do so.

The upshot: If you can find a way to align *your* self-interests with *others'* self-interests, it's highly likely you will be able to get them to support your actions and wishes.

Once you've found connections and links between your goals and the goals of the other parties, you want to take the next step by demonstrating to those people the connections—the enlightened self-interests that exist, and the opportunities they present for everyone involved.

As noted, direct alignment tends to be easy to spot. That said, we find that top ultra-wealthy entrepreneurs are very process-oriented. For example, some of them will create a grid or matrix (or at least a list) specifying where the overlap between the two sets of goals exists.

In situations where direct alignment doesn't exist or where you want to further enhance the relationship, look for ways to deliver added value that can help others achieve their goals that don't directly line up with yours. When you do this, they'll be strongly inclined to help you succeed.

When delivering added value, there's usually a need to think about the resources and capabilities you can provide and how they can be used to help others achieve their self-interests. This is much more an art than a science. Some tools used by some ultra-wealthy entrepreneurs to help them decide what's added value include brainstorming, mind mapping and structured analytics.

Success tip: Central to the Everyone Wins Process is that its effectiveness is squarely on your shoulders. Don't expect other people to take the same approach. Because relatively few people are adept at enhancing and optimizing business relationships, you becoming skilled gives you an astounding competitive advantage.

Regardless of your approach, consider doing what the best ultra-wealthy entrepreneurs often do to make all this work: Put together a plan for *each* of the people with whom you have a business relationship. The plan can be entirely in your head, or you can explicitly lay it out and document it.

Most effective plans consist of the answers to the following six questions:

What is in my self-interests in this specific situation?

What do I want out of this relationship in the short term and the longer term?

What are his or her self-interests?

What can I do to help this person achieve his or her self-interests?

How do I best frame my recommendations and advice and offer support?

How do I ask for support so I can achieve my self-interests?

Again, for each and every business relationship you seek to enhance or optimize, you can go through these six questions. Doing so will help you get clear on the relationship's worth to you and what you can and are willing to do to enhance it. You'll also be more comfortable about asking for the support you need.

These six questions are the cornerstones of personal wealth creation coaching. By using them to help think through and refine your actions, you're able to make nearly any relationship you choose much more meaningful. This is true whether you want to move someone up the business relationship hierarchy or just maximize the relationship in a specific set of circumstances.

Framing: Positioning your self-interests

The process of structuring and articulating perspectives and viewpoints so they strongly resonate with others is known as framing. Very often framing can be just as important as the substance of the message. In other words, *how* you say something can be just as important as *what* you say. In negotiations, for example, even identical bargaining positions can elicit very different responses from the other side based on how they are framed.

Framing is all about making sense. It helps people better understand and relate to what you're suggesting, such as why your recommendations will help them achieve their goals. It is the psychological context used to create greater agreement between you and them.

Framing is how you get agreement when you show the commonalities in everyone's enlightened self-interests. It's how you deliver added value and leverage the Law of Reciprocity. It's how you can get the best responses when you're asking for support.

Success tip: Those in the upper echelon of ultra-wealthy entrepreneurs prove to be very adept at framing their discussions and focusing on the other person. They are always working hard to make the conversation about the person sitting across from them and not about themselves and their interests (which they often intentionally keep in the background). You need to do the same.

One effective framing technique involves the **self-interests framework** we first discussed in **Chapter 10** (see Exhibit 12.1). This framework can help you gain and categorize insights and perspectives about what really does and does not matter to other people. Consider each category, and construct your recommendation based on what you learned.

- **Their goals and objectives.** You want to show the other party the ways you will help them reach their goals and objectives. You might be focusing on delivering added value so they can attain their intermediary goals. Whatever your guidance or request, tie it to how you're helping them reach their goals (especially their end goals).

- **Their critical concerns.** You always need to be cognizant of and often address what's most important to them presently. Your ability to show how commonalities in agendas or how your added value will translate into their being able to better deal with their critical concerns is incredibly powerful.

- **Their self-image.** You want to align your suggestions and intentions with their self-image. By doing so, you signify respect and you also get agreement. For example, you can find areas where you're in agreement with some positive aspect or quality they see in themselves, and you can bring it into the conversation as appropriate.

- **The logic of their key positions with supporting evidence.** By using the rationales and facts they rely on, you're using the very same foundations they're using. It's about capitalizing on their strongly held beliefs. The more you can point to their experiences and their logic in support of your recommendations, for instance, the less resistance you'll encounter.

Different approaches to framing

There are many ways to frame conversations using a wide variety of strategies, tactics, tools and techniques. Two approaches that tend to work very well for (and are favorites of) top ultra-wealthy entrepreneurs are causality and storytelling.

Causality

Causality is very direct. This is the basic formula for causality:

What + why + how = further enhanced business relationship

- *What* describes what a business associate wants to achieve. It is often about their incremental goals. An example is starting a new line of products at the company or getting the board to provide more stock options.

- *Why* is the justification for these goals. For instance, they're the reasons they believe a new line of products makes sense or the rationale for getting more stock options. When addressing the why, you also can help allay their insecurities, reinforce their self-image or highlight their abilities.

- *How* is your added value or where there's direct alignment. It's not enough to be reassuring; you have to do something that moves the needle. For instance, you can make a connection to someone who has worked in setting up a new line of products or someone who can demonstrate that the person is undercompensated. How is the nature of your added value, or it's where the overlap is.

Put *what, why* and *how* together smartly and you will enhance the business relationship. As you're helping others achieve their self-interests, you can ask for what you need in order to achieve your self-interests.

It helps to get feedback when applying causality. One way to do this is by attaching confirming questions to your recommendations or requests. Examples include:

- "Is this making sense to you?"
- "Are you good with things?"
- "Are we going in the right direction?"
- "Does this sound right?"
- "Are there any problems with this?"

Tier-one ultra-wealthy entrepreneurs extensively use causality, as it's the easiest and most straightforward approach.

Storytelling

The ability to bring people together by weaving engaging stories is very powerful. The more absorbing the story, the stronger its impact. That is, the more people are psychologically involved, the more likely it is the story will motivate them to action.

Effective storytelling is a topic that is beyond the scope of this book. However, we want to make sure you understand how to set the stage so your narrative about achieving success resonates with your business associates. Thus, they will see clearly how those same courses of action will benefit them.

Two very effective ways to set the stage are fostering wishful identification and visioning the future.

Fostering wishful identification. Good storytelling draws on the storyteller's experiences and insights to convey a message or course of action that produces results. In addition, you want to bring the listeners into your story. Your aim is to have them identify with the star character in the story and relate the story to what they are concerned about and dealing with. You can accomplish this by beginning your story with phrases such as:

- "Just like you …"
- "I was once in a situation very similar to the one you're describing, and …"

- "Let me tell you about my experience with a partner just like your partner …"

Telling stories that connect with the issues your business associates are facing—and that have positive outcomes—creates *wishful identification.* People want to be the star character in the story—the one who gets the happy ending. Just as the character in the story attains success, they now see it as their turn to succeed. The story tells them that the outcomes they want are possible if they do what the character did—i.e., take the action steps that you are advising them to take.

Visioning the future. Another way to set the stage is to tell a story depicting a bright and prosperous future. In such a story, you paint a picture of the future where some (maybe even all) of the self-interests of the other person are realized. Some phrases that can be useful to start this type of story include:

- "Picture this …"
- "What would happen if …"
- "Imagine that …"
- "Think of a world where …"
- "Looking into the future, I can see …"

You then describe the attainment of some or all of their self-interests, provided they follow your recommendations. These stories also should have happy endings, of course.

These approaches are certainly not exclusive of each other. On the contrary, they (and other approaches) often are best used in conjunction. The approach or approaches you choose will depend on the circumstances.

What's more, there are a lot of ways you can frame your recommendations, advice and requests. We've briefly told you about two of them—causality and storytelling—that we see commonly being used by those ultra-wealthy entrepreneurs enjoying the highest levels of success.

For any framing technique to fit in with the Everyone Wins Process, it must meet two conditions:

- **The framing techniques must be effective.** No one wants to use something that doesn't work.
- **The framing techniques must be used to help your business associates achieve their self-interests.** Doing so smartly and elegantly also will result in their helping you achieve your self-interests.

Getting results by gaining commitments

Consistency is a societal adaptive mechanism. It enables other people to act knowing what to expect from people they're dealing with. Without consistency or predictability, our lives would be completely fragmented and erratic. What's more, people who are inconsistent and erratic are often seen by others as less intelligent or even emotionally troubled.

By understanding everyone's self-interests, you can help others take actions that benefit all. Tactically, it is often very useful when you get them to make commitments. When businesspeople make commitments, they're taking a stand. Most people will then act in accord with their stated stand.

Because most people psychologically strive to be consistent, they match their thinking and behavior to their self-image. If your business associates think of themselves in a certain way, then they will act in a way that doesn't disrupt that self-image. For example, if someone's self-image includes being highly compassionate, that person is more likely to follow your advice and make a commitment if you can show that your recommendations prove he or she is indeed compassionate.

In accord with the Everyone Wins Process, the method is straightforward (**Exhibit 12.2**):

- You already have identified their self-interests.
- You now pinpoint how they can commit to a course of action or an intended outcome.
- You ask them to make the commitment.

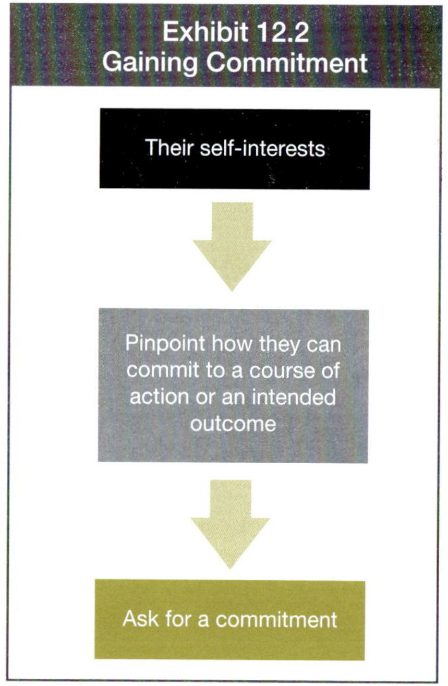

There are different ways to ask for the commitment. You can be direct, like this:

> *"Let's bring in the consultants I recommended."*

> *"Please connect me with the different vendors we discussed."*

If the other person agrees, you have commitment. An often-superior approach is to use questions. In the process of using questions, you are well served by accenting the other's self-interests:

> *"Because you're interested in changing the strategic direction, would it make sense to bring in the consultants I suggested?"*

> *"You want to meet the people at the research firm. If I can set that up, would you help me connect with the different vendors we discussed?"*

Pro tip: Keep the long game in mind. Chances are you'll get greater and greater commitment as you interact with the same people over time. Knowing what matters to them and how that coincides with your agenda, you can get consistently better at strategically asking for their commitment to various courses of action.

Advice: Start with small requests tied to their self-interests. When they act as you recommend—helping them and you—they're making a commitment. In future situations, you can make larger and larger requests. All these requests help them achieve their self-interests. Moreover, they are psychologically making a greater and greater commitment. It then becomes much harder to not follow through.

A word about ethics

Very early in this book, we explained that the Everyone Wins Process is very easy to learn and amazingly effective. Because you've read to this point, we're confident you've picked up concepts, ideas and actionable strategies that you can use to become more successful.

Remember how the process came together. We used ethnographic research, observing the habits and actions of the ultra-wealthy over two decades. Those efforts enabled us to discern and organize the best practices of the most successful ultra-wealthy entrepreneurs in terms of their business dealings. We dissected how this select group enhances and optimizes business relationships, and we put our findings together in an orderly, logical and reproducible format. We've found that when entrepreneurs do adopt the Everyone Wins Process, their results tend to motivate them to become more and more capable, and more and more successful.

But we also emphasized that the Everyone Wins Process is highly ethical. This really comes down to you. It's our strong belief that integrity matters. Integrity matters enormously.

We acknowledge that the Everyone Wins Process can be corrupted. We've seen entrepreneurs use components of the process and turn into grifters.

But because successful entrepreneurship is about playing the long game, we have found that using a despoiled version of the Everyone Wins Process eventually leads to business and personal failures in most cases. Instead of enhancing or optimizing business relationships, grifters end up with the people in those relationships turning against them at a moment's notice. Over time, the bad reputation of these grifters will precede them—and few people will want to work with them.

We strongly believe the most important component of the Everyone Wins Process is your integrity. Being ethical makes good business sense and makes for a better society. But it's up to you to bring integrity to the process.

Of course, all of your actions don't mean much if there aren't great outcomes to back them up. Next, we address how to track and assess results—the results you're helping others get and the results they're delivering to you—so you can determine the effectiveness of your efforts.

CHAPTER 13

Accelerate Success by Tracking Results

Good intentions and a strong work ethic are noble traits that every entrepreneur should possess. However, good intentions and hard work are actually of limited importance unless they generate successful results.

Ultra-wealthy entrepreneurs, for example, are not inclined to stay with an initiative once they're confident it's not going to pay off. While they'll persevere through adversity, they tend to be good at knowing when to shift gears and move on.

As you use the Everyone Wins Process, you'll have to answer the following questions on an ongoing basis:

Am I getting the results I want?

Are my business associates getting the results they want?

How do I know whether people are achieving their self-interests?

Always remember that the Everyone Wins Process is designed to help you and your business associates achieve your respective and shared goals. Therefore, as you apply the Everyone Wins Process, you need to clearly track how everyone is doing. Tracking results will help you assess your efforts and show where you need to refine your approach to produce better results.

Another advantage to tracking results: You can leverage your success at helping others reach their goals to further incentivize them to help you achieve your self-interests.

Finally, by tracking results, you're well prepared for when a business associate comes at you with a "what have you done for me lately?" attitude. Armed with evidence of concrete results you helped generate, you can quickly address this pushback—and even use it to your advantage.

Let's briefly look at some ways top ultra-wealthy entrepreneurs tend to track their outcomes.

When tracking results matter

The Everyone Wins Process has a different form and texture in different professional environments. To exemplify this, we'll touch on four scenarios.

Scenario 1: Working with other entrepreneurs

With other business owners, the Everyone Wins Process usually results in ways to deliver added value. For most entrepreneurs, their self-interests often revolve around building great companies and becoming seriously wealthy.

Tracking the outcomes entrepreneurs achieve through the added value you give them lets you know what to ask of them (and even how best to ask). When you are able to point to the big results you've helped them achieve, the Law of Reciprocity usually kicks into high gear.

Scenario 2: Negotiating with government officials

When it comes to optimizing relationships with government officials, the Everyone Wins Process is the same. The big difference is usually that the self-interests of government officials are substantially different from those of entrepreneurs.

When working with government officials, your aim typically should be to find areas of commonality and direct alignment. This will include pursuing results that are consistent with certain policies. Optics plays a big role, as does process. Entrepreneurs sometimes struggle with this, especially when a particular path seems so logical. Yet, if you understand this and are patient, all the other lessons will be applicable. Delivering added value does occur, but not often. It's usually about making sure the government gets what it needs and wants, and that there is a somewhat predictable process. Then you can achieve your agenda concurrently.

By tracking results, you show the government officials that you're concerned about doing what's right. This builds credibility and therefore makes it easier and more efficient the next time you need to deal with government bureaucracies.

Scenario 3: Leading a growing company

Ideally, you want your employees to act as powerful advocates and give their all to make the company shine. Here, both direct alignment and delivering added value are possibilities.

You want to make all employees individually successful and in sync with the vision and objectives of the company. If you're able to show them how following you will enable them to achieve their own objectives, they'll be incredibly supportive.

Scenario 4: Personal wealth creation coaching

An interesting aspect of personal wealth creation coaching (see **Appendix B**) is that the results are evident. If you seek out a wealth creation coach and are accepted into the program, it's easy to determine whether that coach has helped you hit your financial end goals within the desired time frame. That said, staying on track and moving forward can be tough if you hit a rough patch. By tracking key incremental progress—for example, every $10 million increase in net worth on the way to the goal of $50 million—you can better remain on course.

Assessing your results

The mechanics of tracking results is straightforward. Using outside sources of information, updates from the people you're dealing with or both, you ascertain the outcomes others are getting. One effective method is to once again ask open-ended questions about the status of things, such as these:

- "How is the project working out?"
- "Where are you with the negotiation?"
- "How did the ideas we discussed play out when you spoke with your partner?"
- "What's working out for you, and what isn't?"

- "What are the obstacles that are getting in the way of your being more successful?"

Getting others to fill you in on their status is usually quite easy.

Next, you need to learn whether they're making adequate progress. Their results need to meet (or exceed) their expectations in order for them to feel they are meeting their goals.

The most successful ultra-wealthy entrepreneurs tend to use a simple mental algorithm when they're delivering added value. They know the other person's self-interest, and they know how they're helping. They also know the level of success. The more success, the more they skillfully bring up their contributions to the person's great results.

Ongoing evaluation

You track results so you can refine your approach to enhancing and optimizing business relationships and accelerate everyone's success. That is, you're doing this with a purpose.

Your ability to enhance and optimize business relationships is going to be lessened unless you're attentively tracking results. As we said, by knowing how much you're helping your business associates achieve their self-interests, you're better positioned to ask for assistance in achieving your goals.

In order to continually further enhance your business relationships—even already optimal relationships—you must track results. Moreover, you must regularly but diplomatically communicate the ways you've helped your business associates achieve their self-interests.

This is similar to the relationship between discovery and empathy. It's not enough for you to know you understand someone; that person must know and sincerely believe you understand him or her. Otherwise, your relationship will be inclined to drift and weaken.

In the next section, we look at what can easily derail your ability to enhance and optimize business relationships. We also look at what happens when you find yourself dealing with unreasonable people—and what you can do about that challenging situation.

PART III

When It Gets Harder

Make no mistake: Implementing the Everyone Wins Process is not a cakewalk. It takes focus, hard work and the ability to react quickly and decisively to information. There are many ways to get tripped up.

In this section, we address some of the more common stumbling blocks and risks that we see when entrepreneurs use the Everyone Wins Process. Some are targeted—such as when entrepreneurs struggle to get their business associates to open up to them during discovery so they can get the information they need in order to move forward. Others are larger in scope—such as what happens when business owners find themselves face-to-face with a monstrous person who is just as likely to try to ruin them as to work in partnership with them.

Regardless, you'll learn ways to address and overcome the problems so you can become increasingly adept at using the Everyone Wins Process to help yourself and others.

CHAPTER 14

When People Are Not Inclined to Share

As we discussed in **Chapter 10: Engage in Discovery to Identify Wants and Needs**, discovery is essential to learning about people. There are times, however, when people are reticent about sharing information. It might be because they feel doing so could put them at a disadvantage. Maybe they're embarrassed by their answers.

Whatever the reason, some people are cagey instead of accessible and forthcoming—especially when the stakes are high, such as in a critical negotiation.

Ask yourself these questions:

Have I ever been in business situations where people were just not into sharing?

How often have I dodged questions people asked me?

What would likely happen if I were able to get people to open up when they otherwise wouldn't?

The Everyone Wins Process is dependent on your discerning your self-interests and those of your business associates. When people are being uncommunicative, it becomes more difficult to do that.

With that in mind, consider some strategies that can help you get people to open up when they're not inclined to tell you what you need to know.

Smart guesswork

As we discussed in **Chapter 10**, open-ended questions are a key part of discovery. But you don't have to rely on them to capture important information. Instead, you can promote sharing in ways that overcome guardedness and get the key insights you want.

The idea is to make calculated, educated assumptions about others—smart guesswork—supported by a set of techniques or prompts (**Exhibit 14.1**). Then you can use follow-up questions and empathy to confirm or deny your educated assumptions.

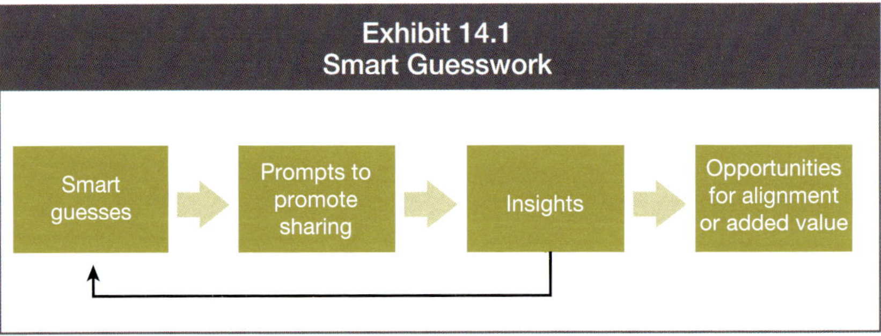

When it comes to soliciting information through smart guesswork, certain themes are consistently effective:

- **Health and well-being.** Anxiety about health is the norm, not the exception, these days. Most people are very concerned about their own and their loves ones' health and well-being. Understanding a person's medical issues, including any specifics and their level of concern, can prove useful in determining his or her priorities.

- **Family matters.** Developments in the lives of those we hold dear can be instrumental in how we end up approaching business endeavors. For most people, when their children have serious issues, business concerns are pushed aside. Knowing about another person's family—especially when there are complications—can be very useful when it comes to doing business with that person.

- **The true state of business and financial affairs.** While most entrepreneurs tend to be upbeat about their business and its prospects, the reality of the situation may be very different. By gaining a more accurate understanding of another person's business and financial affairs, you're better able to see ways to help him or her as well as yourself.

Focusing your discovery efforts on these and other themes, you can solicit insights about people and their situations. For example, people in their 50s and older are more likely than younger individuals to have various medical concerns. One ultra-wealthy, over-50 entrepreneur we know had a physician put together a chart showing the ages at which various health issues tend to arise. The physician also set out the nature and speed of incapacitation caused by each health issue.

The ultra-wealthy entrepreneur used the age of his business associates, combined with careful observations, to get them talking about their medical concerns. This approach allowed the entrepreneur to find commonality with others and build greater rapport with them over various health issues and concerns. Ultimately, that rapport and “bonding” helped the entrepreneur close more deals with more favorable terms than he would have gotten otherwise.

Another example: The more children a person has, the more likely he or she is to have a child with health or behavioral problems. Of course, having only one child can sometimes be just as problematic. Still, knowing the number of children business associates have can set the stage for discussions of expenses they need to meet and problems they need to take care of.

And while your business associates may be outwardly very positive about their companies’ fortunes, they may actually be quite concerned. Talking about current, specific problems in the economy, for instance, can trigger more honest conversations about the fortunes of each person’s company.

Even when your smart guesses are off base, which they will be now and again, they’re still helpful because they’ll enable you to quickly move in a more fruitful direction.

Ultimately, making good guesses involves thinking about the odds given what you know about people or demographic groups similar to the person in front of you at the moment.

These themes can be the jumping-off points for you to learn more about those in your business relationships. When they share this kind of information, they’ll be increasingly likely to share other information. Moreover, once they’re somewhat comfortable and begin to trust you, you’ll likely find them more responsive to your open-ended questions.

Pro tip: Gently touching on topics that are meaningful to them and have emotional weight will usually start or move conversations along. You then need to be very sensitive to the content and not push but impactfully listen well and be highly empathetic.

Facilitating sharing

Once you make your smart guesses, it's time to break out the verbal prompts—statements and questions to verify your guesses and to get the other person to share information. Here are three examples.

1. **Make a statement that's somewhat ill-defined.** These are statements, often truisms, that come across as accurate. You use them to elicit a positive response while leaving room for the other person to fill in the gaps. For example:

   - "It tends to be difficult finding enough time for your family and running your business."
   - "As we get older, we get to see the inside of the doctor's office more and more."
   - "Dealing with the ways technology keeps changing the industry is a struggle."

2. **Use generalization about most people to kick-start sharing.** Sometimes you can use generalized character statements or observations that most people would say describe them accurately.

   Examples include:

   - "It sounds like it would be nice if more people appreciated your efforts."
   - "You're on target for most of your goals, but you have to make a concerted effort every day."

- "It's hard to manage everything on your plate."

3. **Use accompanying questions.** Accompanying questions are conversational questions tacked onto a declarative statement. While many times they're closed-ended questions, they usually spark conversation as people follow their answers with sharing. Examples of accompanying questions (in italics) include:

    - "These days, more and more parents are worried about their kids' future. It's a different world today. *Wouldn't you agree?*

    - "A lot of people in the industry are very concerned that their companies are going to be hit with more personnel problems. *Does that sound right?*"

    - "High blood pressure, prediabetes, changing liver test scores… it seems that everyone has health issues. *Are you seeing this too?*"

These kinds of prompts are designed to motivate the people you're dealing with to share information about themselves. It's a subtle and often fairly low-profile way of collecting facts, opinions and perspectives that can be effective when asking open-ended questions causes others to pull back.

You can always learn about others

As long as your business associates are willing to talk with you, there are methodologies you can use to help them share. For example, the main intention of smart guesswork is to better understand the businesspeople you're dealing with even when they're somewhat reticent.

By understanding their major concerns and priorities (and the whys behind them) you can uncover self-interests. By gaining a deeper understanding of what's important to someone else, you're able to identify ways you can be helpful and thereby enhance or optimize the business relationship.

Of course, sometimes enhancing and optimizing relationships becomes challenging not because of the reticence of others to share but rather because of your own problematic attitudes and actions. In the next chapter, you'll discover some key ways that you can potentially stumble in your efforts—and how to sidestep those errors.

CHAPTER 15

The Challenges of the Three E's—Egos, Emotions and Energy

It takes time and effort to enhance business relationships. It's even more work to build relationships that stand firmly in the strong and optimal categories of the business relationship hierarchy, as we discussed in **Chapter 2**.

That makes sense. People are rarely going to trust you just because you tell them you're trustworthy. Trust is built over time as you learn more about others and deliver support consistently. People will trust you when you prove by your repeated actions that you're trustworthy.

Along the way, it can be easy to stumble. Ask yourself these questions.

Have I ever almost desperately wanted credit or recognition for something I did that was in fact monumental?

Have I ever been so angry during a negotiation that I wanted to shake some sense into someone on the other side?

Have I ever been so down that I caused my business associates to become discouraged as well?

If you responded yes, then you're in the vast majority of entrepreneurs—and this is one case where you would very much prefer to be in the minority

When the problem is you

When we struggle to enhance and optimize our business relationships, often we find that the problem getting in your way is ourselves. So it's paramount that we examine some of the key ways we sabotage our efforts so we can avoid those mistakes.

We've found that the three most common ways to fail are needing to have your ego stroked, not being in control of your emotions and lacking energy. Many times, these causes of failure interact. Let's start with ego.

Your ego needs stroking

Among the following choices, what is more important to you?

- Being right, or achieving your self-interests?
- Having other people sing your praises, or achieving your self-interests?
- Getting people to see you as smart (or caring, talented, etc.), or achieving your self-interests?

Sometimes, you can get both outcomes. But when you have to make a choice, what do you choose?

The top ultra-wealthy entrepreneurs we have worked with and coached are extremely disciplined about choosing amazing outcomes over having their egos stroked. They understand that they cannot deposit ego in the bank. Getting credit and being told how great they are is meaningless compared with getting substantial results that meet their definition of winning. They'll even downplay themselves and their contributions if doing so makes it easier to get the results they most want.

This is no small feat. It's easy to let our egos sometimes get the better of us. Social reinforcement of our self-image, for example, is a powerful reward for most people. That can be especially true if you've accomplished great things. But ego commonly conflicts with getting ideal outcomes—such as a better price when you sell your company, having business associates introduce you to people who can make you more successful and attaining the loyalty of your employees.

Among the most successful ultra-wealthy entrepreneurs, the answer is usually not recognition. It's about garnering greater business success. And having their egos stroked is a poor alternative to achieving better business outcomes.

Top entrepreneurs are able to push ego aside because they make the conscious effort to emphasize and focus on others and not themselves. The underlying principle of the Everyone Wins Process—and what makes it so very powerful—is that you focus outwardly, on *others*:

- Their wants
- Their expressed and latent needs
- Their self-image

- Their anxieties and insecurities
- Their definition of winning

This leaves very little space for your own ego to take over and drive the situation.

Of course, you continue to keep your own self-interests at the front of your mind—but obscured from the people you're dealing with. Your goal is to put your energies into understanding their self-interests, finding where there are enlightened self-interests and discovering how to help them succeed in ways that will also fuel your own success.

The reverse: Positive recognition and "ego stroking" may be very important to certain people. They may want to be perceived as the alpha. For some, it's about "proof" that they're big shots in the big leagues.

This can work to your advantage if you determine that you can better enhance or optimize the relationship if you stroke their egos. That absolutely doesn't mean being patronizing. Instead, you're looking for qualities, attributes and capabilities in these people that you truly find impressive. You're looking for the things they did that you consider notable, then making sure *they know* that you see their positive features and successes.

Negative emotions run amok

Because of the actions of your business associates, there are times you're likely going to feel angry, frustrated, discouraged, nervous, anxious, irritated, scared, exasperated and more.

Your feelings may be completely justified, but you cannot let them translate into actions that diminish your ability to enhance or optimize these relationships. Running amok, negative emotions can ruin your ability to build rapport and achieve greater professional and personal success.

Succumbing to emotional reactions usually means you're not thinking things through as best you can. Consequently, you're probably going to make bad judgments that will only further complicate matters.

When negative emotions get the better of you, everything can quickly spiral downward. Say you're frustrated with your business partner. You're not thinking clearly, and you say something that antagonizes the other person, diminishing the chances of getting what you want. It's something you cannot easily take back. Your relationship is damaged, and it will probably take time and work to repair it.

The big culprit here? Among entrepreneurs, we've found that one of the more common adverse emotional reactions is anger. Becoming angry is fairly common in intense business environments. Angry individuals tend to overreact, blowing issues out of proportion and distracting from the important considerations at hand. Some people equate angry outbursts with power. They see ranting and raving as showing who's in charge. The reality is that anger usually demonstrates helplessness and frustration. It often shows weakness in actions and character. That means you need to keep your anger in check and deal with situations in a calm, objective and disciplined manner.

People who are demonstrably angry very often cut off other available options. They box themselves in and thereby hurt their position and the likelihood of achieving their self-interests.

One key to successfully mitigating intense anger or other strong emotions: ***Don't take it personally***. You never want someone else to be pushing your buttons or pulling your strings.

As much as possible, stay calm and poised. This conveys that you are in control of your life, and it can help de-escalate overwrought situations when others are tense and acting out.

Even if someone is acting like a high school bully, avoid acting defensively. If the person makes inaccurate comments designed to inflame the proceedings, once again ask yourself, "Would I rather be right, or would I rather win?" Then take a breath and be patient. This likely will take some willpower, as most people in these types of situations want to justify their actions or positions and defend themselves. For some people, it's a matter of principle.

Most of the top ultra-wealthy entrepreneurs have a strong sense of self-worth coupled with knowledge of their self-interests. By keeping those two things foremost in their minds at all times, they can pretty easily rein in disruptive responses to the negative emotions they feel. And because they probably have little respect for bullies, they tend not to take abrasive comments personally at all.

Pro tip: One of the very best ways you can respond to anger is to not respond at all. Such a reaction can be very unsettling; it often makes hotheads even hotter. If you're then able to show some alignment of their goals and your goals or deliver added value, you probably will be seen as even more useful to them. The more useful they see you as being, the more likely they'll be receptive to ways to help you achieve your goals and agenda. Think of their uncontrolled emotions as opportunities to make yourself essential to their aims.

A lack of energy

While others can be drawn to you because of your high energy and can-do perspective, they're likely to move away if you exhibit low energy and a can't-do attitude.

In just about every situation, you need to be upbeat and positive, and your energy level needs to be high. However, if you are over-the-top upbeat and positive, you're usually not going to be taken seriously. If there are complications in a situation, for example, being unrealistically optimistic will only hurt your credibility. Better to set out the specific complications, reiterate your vision or solutions and be very reassuring that following your recommendations will produce desired outcomes.

Ultimately, your self-assurance is a big factor in your ability to persevere and bring others into your orbit. It's the positive energy you need to bring to enhance or optimize your business relationships. Think about it from the perspective of leadership. If you're not excited about your company's mission and strategy, why would anyone working for you be motivated to give it their all?

This carries over to both negotiations and networking. In making a deal with someone—say, selling your company—you want to be tremendously excited about the prospects of the business. This will make the other side want even more to do the deal. In networking, you want to be seen as successful and energized, as other businesspeople gravitate to people with those traits.

Your enthusiasm can make those around you feel better about themselves. The rationale behind this is that by believing in yourself and what you are saying, you're helping others reduce their own level of anxiety and uncertainty as well as mitigate their insecurities. It helps convey that you have the answers they're looking for.

Success tip: People prefer optimists and their positive attitude that good things are going to happen. Optimism helps many get through the hard times. Being upbeat and enthusiastic seeds optimism.

The reverse: When others are unenthusiastic or, worse, depressed, and you can show them a path to accomplishing their goals, they'll want to align themselves with you. Your high-energy, can-do attitude can help them power through their negative feelings. Inside, everyone desires growth. Moreover, as you respond empathetically—recognizing people's feelings and the reasons for them—they will usually open up more, enabling you to gain more insights so you can find commonalities and better deliver added value.

You're in control

Remember that you're likely in control when trying to enhance or optimize your business relationships. If you're one of the select entrepreneurs to adopt the approach and ideas we've presented in this book, you can set the stage and call the shots to a large degree.

When you focus on the self-interests of everyone, you create a kind of buffer that keeps your ego and emotions in check and helps you convey positivity and energy to those around you. That in turn can help you enhance or optimize just about any business relationship, deliver the results you want—and help ensure that everyone comes away feeling like winners.

All that said, the Everyone Wins Process doesn't guarantee a clear, easy and smooth path to results. The fact is, you're going to encounter people along the way who are just plain difficult to deal with. When that happens—and it will—you need to be ready to steer those difficult people in the direction you want them to go. We'll tackle that in the next chapter.

The approach of ultra-wealthy entrepreneurs

Many of the most successful ultra-wealthy entrepreneurs tell us it took time for them to avoid having knee-jerk reactions. In the beginning, they had to literally stop and think. They had to question the value of reacting the way they wanted to at that moment. Only then were they able to put their egos aside or stay calm and composed. It is a very conscious and awkward process.

These ultra-wealthy entrepreneurs also made it clear that by making self-interests central, they can dig deep when necessary to muster the positive energies that help keep everyone meaningfully engaged. It's hard to stay positive all the time. But it can make a profound difference in how business associates react to your recommendations and ideas.

Over time, these top ultra-wealthy entrepreneurs discovered it became much more natural to ensure that their egos and negative emotions always stayed under control and they got others excited about what was beneficial to them. It took awareness, discipline and practice. You can do the same thing. You initially want to increase your reaction time so you can respond in ways that serve your self-interest.

CHAPTER 16

Dealing with Difficult People

Because business relationships are so vital to your success as an entrepreneur, you're almost certainly going to meet and need to work with a lot of people over the years. Most people you meet in business are hardworking and caring. Few relish schadenfreude—taking pleasure in other people failing.

Still, ask yourself these questions:

Have I ever met someone in business who thinks the whole wide world revolves around him or her?

Do I have business relationships with people who believe getting the results they want justifies nearly any actions they take?

Do I have business relationships with people who are adamant about their points of view even when logic and facts are not on their side?

It's a given that successful entrepreneurs—and that includes you—will have to deal with difficult people. As you build your business, you're going to have to work with (and sometimes work around) people who make things unnecessarily hard. The thing is, dealing with difficult people can still (sometimes) enable you to achieve your interests while simultaneously helping them get closer to their goals.

That means it can pay—literally—to understand difficult people better, know when it does and doesn't make sense to work with them, and use the right tactics to pursue your self-interests in the appropriate situations.

The many varieties of difficult people

There are several distinct types of difficult people you're likely to encounter on your entrepreneurial journey:

- **Fools** do not think critically. Logic is not their forte and therefore not a way for you to connect with them. For example, many fools are prone to believe in off-the-charts conspiracy theories, which makes it hard to negotiate or work with them.

- **Narcissists** see everything revolving around them—they're the ones and often the only ones who can make things happen, at least in their minds. They strive to project an image of supreme self-confidence and likely see themselves as hyperintelligent, attractive and incredibly capable. Anyone or anything that calls their self-image into question is simply wrong.

- **Subclinical psychopaths** present themselves as caring and likable, but their charm is superficial and underpinned by a lack of empathy. They can be callous and will have no problem throwing you under the bus in a business situation. (They might even make sure the bus rolls over you a few times.)

- **Machiavellians** are cunning, deceitful and all-around manipulative. They figure out precisely what you want and create an illusion for delivering on that desire. They are exceptional at "selling" hope and accomplishments, while always failing to deliver.

- **Zealots** are fanatics. They have extreme belief systems that are incontrovertible and unchallengeable. No matter what the situation or circumstance, they adhere to their belief system even when there is strong, solid evidence to the contrary. They find it completely unacceptable if you don't agree with them.

Difficult people can make it very problematic for you to achieve your self-interests. Their attitude and approaches to negotiating, for example, can make it nearly impossible to get a deal done. For example, if the other side is negotiating an agreement giving you much of what you want but you know they have a history of not following through, you have to take that fact into account.

We can offer a few pieces of advice that are true regardless of the type of difficult person:

1. **Don't rely on reason.** The idea of reasoning with a difficult person might sound good, but it can easily lead to tremendous frustration and aggravation. Concentrating on logic and the specifics of the issues is not going get results for you or them. A good fact-filled argument can be useless.

2. **Don't try to optimize your relationship with a difficult person.** In **Chapter 2: The Business Relationship Hierarchy**, we talked about different levels of relationships. Most relationships with difficult people are usually weak but can sometimes be strong. It's nearly

impossible to build optimal relationships with difficult people. There are usually just too many issues that prevent the relationship from reaching the pinnacle. Instead, you'll seek to enhance the relationship situationally within the particular category.

3. **Expect to work hard.** Winning when dealing with difficult people is going to take a lot more work than is required when enhancing relationships with others. Recognize that you will need to spend a great deal of time, energy or both—and determine whether it's worth the effort. One area where you'll need to spend some time is identifying the specific type of difficult person you're dealing with. That part of the Everyone Wins Process may require more effort to get the insights you need from your discovery. Likewise, some difficult people want to win at all costs and are very willing to do nearly anything (including pounding you into the ground) to achieve that. It takes a deft hand to avoid being taken down as well as to ensure, for instance, that both parties can close a deal and walk away satisfied.

4. **Don't expect a difficult person to change or become less difficult.** Difficult people are difficult. It's their nature, and their nature is not going to change. One of the biggest mistakes you can make is thinking they will change, grow or evolve. Always remember that difficult people are who they are and will act as they act. The good news: They actually become quite predictable, which can work in your favor. By understanding their psychology, you're able to modify how you behave with them—including how to best apply the Everyone Wins Process in order to achieve your agenda as well as to help them achieve theirs.

To get some more insight into difficult people, consider two of the most common types you are likely to encounter as a business owner: fools and narcissists.

The fool

It's written in 2 Corinthians 11:19 (KJV), "For ye suffer fools gladly, seeing ye yourselves are wise." In other words, put up with fools because you're so smart.

Today, of course, we're warned to not suffer fools gladly—in other words, we should get angry at people we consider unintelligent and confront them about their stupidity.

However, that modern advice may not always make good business sense. Enhancing and optimizing business relationships with fools may be a good strategy in some situations.

Start by recognizing that fools are pervasive—you can find them seemingly everywhere in life and in business.

Their motivations vary. They can be unrealistic, exploitive, convoluted, self-centered, delusional or just plain dumb. In business environments, fools are regularly ruled by their egos and their anxieties. Many seem to have a strong sense of privilege, if not entitlement, for reasons that defy logic.

There are a number of ways to deal with fools (**Exhibit 16.1**) as part of your efforts to enhance relationships and engage in the Everyone Wins Process.

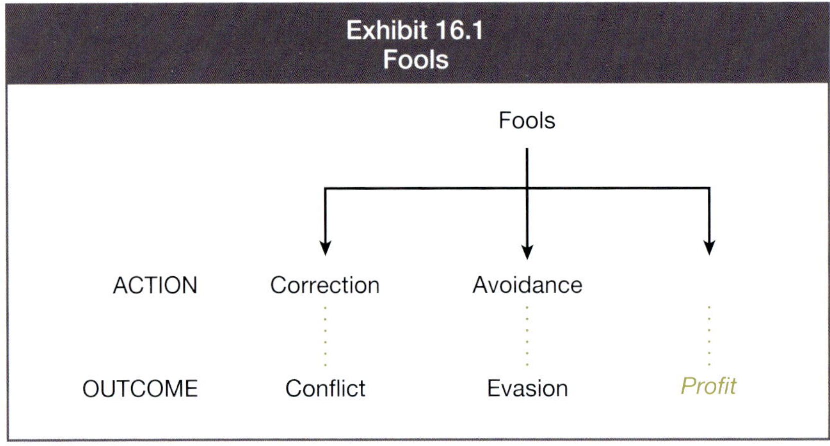

1. Correction

It's common to try to correct fools' perceptions and actions. The idea is that explaining, educating and helping them understand a different point of view will cause them to see things differently—and they no longer will be stupid about the matters at hand.

Unfortunately, this approach usually proves to be naive. Fools by their nature are fools—and as the saying goes, "You can't fix stupid." What's more, fools don't know they *are* fools. Example: People who are part of the Flat Earth movement will not be swayed by any logic or facts you can muster to convince them the world is a sphere.

Trying to correct fools is more likely to lead to confrontations than to a change of position, due to their determination and stubbornness. (It is not uncommon for people to sometimes want to shake or yell at fools. While such action can be cathartic for the other person, it is only likely to reinforce a fool's position.)

Rarely do the wealthiest entrepreneurs engage in correcting fools, as they understand doing so will be a time-consuming and frustrating failure.

2. Avoidance and suffering fools gladly

The other two actions are avoidance and suffering fools gladly. Top ultra-wealthy entrepreneurs tend to adopt one of these two approaches based on their calculation of the relationship value of the fool. For example:

- If the fool can provide little relationship value, he or she is avoided.
- If the fool has high relationship value, then the ultra-wealthy entrepreneur suffers that person gladly all (or nearly all) of the time and work to help the person achieve his or her agenda.

It's more likely than not that fools will control resources and can deliver opportunities when the relationship is enhanced. Consequently, highly successful ultra-wealthy entrepreneurs often capitalize on the preponderance of fools throughout the business world.

The upshot: Fools can be wonderful for your business and personal financial success—if you don't try to change them, if you learn to accept their idiocy and irrationality, and if you use the Everyone wins Process to make them and yourself more successful.

The narcissist

Narcissists are powerful people who make everything all about themselves and see other people as mere tools to use (and abuse, if necessary).

Unfortunately, many very wealthy and powerful people are narcissists. That means you may very well encounter such people on your own path to business success and significant personal wealth. Your ability to work with them when it's in your interest while avoiding being manipulated by them can be instrumental in your success.

The good news: It's pretty easy to spot narcissists and know whom you're dealing with. Everything is about them. All the good is because of them, all the bad is someone else's doing—and everybody should be thankful that they're around to make things right.

Narcissists need to be loved. They desperately need the adulation of other people to prove to themselves they are worthwhile. Their bravado and extreme outward self-confidence are often how they cover up their incredible insecurities and fears. Some of the characteristics of narcissists include:

- A self-image of being unique, special, hyperintelligent, attractive and so on
- A belief that other people envy them and therefore want to hurt them
- An expectation that other people constantly will acknowledge them and provide them with special treatment

Other people and their concerns are secondary to a narcissist's prominence and significance. People are tools, utilities or instruments who support and reinforce the worldview and central role played by the narcissist.

Narcissists also feel an overwhelming urge to push back against each and every slight they feel, no matter how meaningless. With no inner strength to validate their self-worth, they must demean and belittle any and all critics to substantiate their belief that they are very important. They see vengeance—the opportunity to go to war with the "enemy"—as necessary in order to prove they are correct, justified and deserving of the recognition they desperately seek.

The combination of narcissism and a strong drive to achieve often results in very psychologically damaged and dangerous individuals commanding the levers of power—be it in a company or a government. They're able to attract followers because they are not encumbered by principles and will readily say things people want to hear, no matter how absurd. In the minds of their followers, these narcissists are on their side and should be admired for telling the "truth"—and not backing down. This is an intense form of charisma, provided you're at all in agreement with the claims being made.

Narcissists are very adept at emotional manipulation. Guilt, fear and anxiety are all weapons to be wielded so people will follow them. Narcissists can be your best friends, provided you recognize them for their prominence. However, narcissists will turn against former friends and relationships quickly—particularly if those people achieve impressive results that draw attention away from the narcissists. They also are very willing to toss aside people who stop adoring them or are no longer useful.

When narcissists succeed—which they do more than you might think—their successes only reinforce their deluded view of their importance in the world and intensify their need for ever greater attention. Anything that calls into question their legitimacy is a lie or a conspiracy meant to hurt them and their followers.

The implications of all this for you are to always be on guard when dealing with narcissists. They might mimic caring and even empathy—but they do so to find exploitable weaknesses, not to build meaningful relationships.

Winning by losing

If you decide you will deal with (or have to deal with) narcissists, you then have another choice to make. You can confront them by focusing on the issues and striving to help them understand different perspectives. But be warned: Such an approach is almost destined to fail.

To artfully achieve your self-interests and even to help narcissists achieve their self-interests when dealing with them, you need to focus on their psychology. You know what they're all about: They survive on attention, live for adulation and need to be idolized. As part of the Everyone Wins Process, you're actually going to have to support the corrupted view narcissists have of themselves.

Many times, you'll end up "winning by losing." This mean you lose *in comparison with* the narcissist. The aim is to make sure narcissists are (in their minds) the winner in any dealings. They win not necessarily because they come away with a better deal, but instead because they believe that everyone greatly respects them and their deal-making expertise. Meanwhile, you have achieved your main goals and objectives and have won based on your definition of winning.

Effectively dealing with fools, narcissists and other difficult people

Remember that you are in control when using the Everyone Wins Process. It's always your responsibility to finds areas of alignment, identify where compromises are possible and find ways to deliver added value. Rarely are all the issues intractable—even when dealing with difficult people. It's more likely that difficult individuals are intractable but the issues at stake are malleable.

The main new wrinkle in doing so is addressing the difficult person's particular psychology. When dealing with difficult people, it can be as much about the psychological victories they require in order to feel good as it is about their getting traction concerning specific issues. In this regard, you have to be accommodating if you want to win. The difficult people you deal with might have serious delusions—but instead of seeking to correct their misconceptions, you need to go with them and move forward. As we asked you back in **Chapter 15**, what matters more to you: being right, or achieving your self-interests?

For example, it can be sensible to suffer fools gladly. With narcissists, it is about validating their self-image. You might need to highlight their accomplishments and perceptions in order to get them to address matters that are important to you. The ideologies of zealots, for instance, need to be recognized and not questioned. Even better, show how your positions are supported by their belief system.

Tough but doable

Dealing effectively with difficult people is typically a major challenge, but it's one you are likely to be required to take on quite often as an entrepreneur. With the Everyone Wins Process, you can navigate these situations well—thereby increasing the likelihood both you and the difficult person will support each other's goals.

Ultimately, your path to significant business success and serious personal wealth may well be smoother once you understand the different types and natures of difficult people—and bring these insights to your use of the Everyone Wins Process.

Unfortunately, the challenges don't stop with people who are merely difficult. You're also occasionally going to encounter people who can best be described as monsters—and they're in a totally different league. We turn to them next.

CHAPTER 17

Dealing and Not Dealing with Monsters

We strongly believe in enhancing and optimizing business relationships. When you're proficient with the Everyone Wins Process, you can consistently get outcomes where literally everyone wins. You win now and in the future, and you're likely to win bigger than you would otherwise. You may even win in ways you never considered.

With this process, employees, other entrepreneurs, governmental agencies and others win as well. This is possible because you're focusing on finding areas of commonality and ways to deliver added value. As you play the long game (see **Chapter 1: What Is Winning?**), the process frequently produces the best outcomes and often opens the doors to highly advantageous, unanticipated business possibilities. It works exceedingly well when you're dealing with reasonable people.

As you've seen, it's even possible to effectively use the Everyone Wins Process when dealing with difficult people. Even in situations where you're dealing with narcissists, zealots or fools, you can still get great results, and so can they. It's often a little harder to discern their self-interests, and it generally will take more effort on your part to find areas of alignment between their agendas and yours or ways to add value. But you can still come out winning big—and so can they.

But what happens when you encounter someone you'd label a monster? Ask yourself these questions:

Have I ever met people in business who at first are charismatic and charming but who will readily vivisect me if it suits them at the moment?

Do I have business relationships with people who can appear caring and concerned but completely lack empathy?

Do I have business relationships with people who project sincerity but, from my experience and what I've heard, are cruel and exploitive?

We hope you were able to answer no to all of these questions. But we know it's more likely you answered yes to at least one—and if you did, you probably know at least one monster.

The Everyone Wins Process is characteristic of a select group of the most successful ultra-wealthy entrepreneurs—the best of the best.

When you're dealing with monsters, the dynamics that govern the Everyone Wins Process completely change.

There are monsters among us

Consequences that would impact others rarely matter to monsters. Shame, for instance, is an emotion they intellectually understand—thus they can exploit it in others—but almost never feel. Anxiety over possible adverse outcomes is just about nonexistent. It's replaced by risk-return calculations in which they know how to alter the probabilities.

Monsters are predators who are perpetually looking for prey. That means you can quite easily end up being a monster's victim. Recipe for a monster (see **Exhibit 17.1**):

- Take a highly motivated, difficult person.
- Remove any compassion, remorse or guilt.
- Add large doses of ruthlessness.
- Mix in a large helping of malicious cunning.

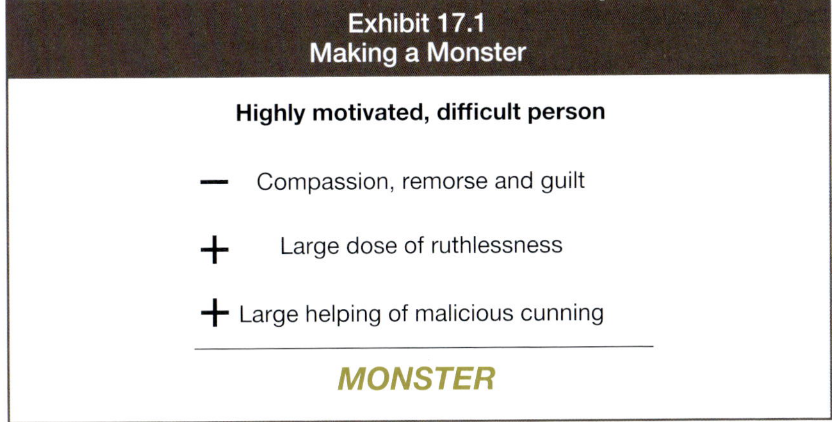

The monsters you tend to meet in business have a strong psychopathic streak. They're also usually quite ingenious, which makes them especially dangerous. This combination of mercilessness and guile can prove disastrous to your business, your personal wealth and your mental stability.

No matter how they might present themselves—and because they're unusually quite crafty, they're able to do an amazing job of impression management—monsters are brutal and cruel. While they can easily come off as charming and caring, it's all an act.

Example: Let's say you want to optimize a business relationship that unbeknownst to you is with a monster. During discovery, you're very likely to find out you could have amazing opportunities from working with this person. You'll also probably discover that there are many ways the two of you are already in sync. However, it's very possible that the interview got turned around so you ended up doing most of the sharing without even realizing it.

The monster is taking what you're sharing and crafting a narrative that you cannot help but find hypnotizing.

It's crystal clear to you that this person can significantly help you achieve your self-interests. Remember, monsters are often astoundingly clever and will carefully spoon-feed you just what you want to hear.

Finding victims

Monsters will also appear to be very empathetic, but what they've really done is weaponize the skills that make up empathy. Monsters are quite expert and practiced at building faux rapport to get others to trust them—before they gut their victims.

The fact is, monsters are particularly adept at determining weaknesses in others (such as insecurities, concerns and anxieties) and exploiting them. Under the guise of being thoughtful and helpful, they can twist, contort and even accentuate others' personal frailties—making people more responsive to and dependent on their solely self-serving advice and guidance.

What's very scary is that monsters are great at pinpointing vulnerabilities and frailties in others and using this information to make those people their victims. When they sense weakness, they are able to use that as a wedge to open up opportunities for themselves—usually at the expense of their victims.

Spotting monsters

In working with and coaching ultra-wealthy entrepreneurs around the world over many decades, we've run into quite a few monsters. Frankly, they're good at hiding their monstrous natures.

The best way to spot them is to pay extremely close attention to their actions. With monsters, it's never what they say that matters—it's only how they behave.

Healthy doses of skepticism and even cynicism can do wonders in helping spot monsters. Think back to President Ronald Reagan, who adopted a Russian proverb—Doveryai, no proveryai (Trust, but verify)—when negotiating with the Russians. It became his signature phrase and is an important lesson that has been strongly embraced by ultra-wealthy entrepreneurs in their business dealings.

If you find someone in a business relationship repeatedly being duplicitous, the klaxons should sound loudly. Unfortunately, this doesn't always happen, as monsters may concoct wonderful stories to explain their actions and cover up lies.

Monsters also will resort to dexterous misdirection whenever they feel pressured. They tend to be very good, for instance, at making people believe they are confused about a situation or misperceive a development instead of what is actually going on—that is, the monster is lying to them. They also often play the martyr and blame everyone around them.

Except for the most brilliant and conniving among them, monsters eventually will unmask themselves. The problem is that too many people ignore the signs for too long.

Success tip: Never let down your guard. When a situation seems too good to be true, it is. If a company savior comes along who claims to be interested only in your well-being and wants only to help—and the person is not a close and loving relative—you might very well be talking to a monster (though sometimes even relatives are monsters).

How to deal with monsters

Referring again to the business relationship hierarchy (see **Chapter 2**), remember that the only kinds of relationships you really can have with monsters are transactional. Even thinking you can move up to a weak relationship with a monster is delusional. The best you can do is further enhance the transactional relationship in a very specific situation. Longer-term relationships are impossible, as monsters don't care about you, and they most likely never will. All that matters to monsters are their own self-interests—period.

The good news: When your agenda and their agenda align, it's actually fairly easy to deal with monsters. In fact, in these circumstances, monsters may be very helpful in moving things along expeditiously. They will use all their skills and resources to help themselves, thereby helping you reach your goals. Monsters are often really good—at least in the short term—at getting results.

The complication—and it's big enough to be a deal breaker in most cases—is that it's very easy for their agendas to deviate from yours, at which point you may quickly become a target and a victim of the monster.

Even minor changes in circumstances can send you and a monster's self-interests in different directions. A character trait of most monsters is that they can quickly shift gears, and before you're aware of it, you've become their prey.

Don't engage

The absolute best way to deal with monsters is not to deal with them at all. Sooner or later, you're very likely to end up as their main course (or at least an appetizer).

Some entrepreneurs believe they can take on monsters. In all probability, this will not turn out well for them. Playing monsters' games is ridiculously hard for most entrepreneurs with even some ethics. Going head-to-head with monsters is bad for two reasons.

1. Monsters are very determined and good at what they do, and most have had lots of practice, so you'd very likely lose any contest. If you try to outthink and outmaneuver them, you'll only further energize them to raise the stakes. Keep in mind that the scariest of monsters are outstandingly capable of bleeding out someone's world. Do you really want to battle a maniacally determined, brutal, pitiless, and probably scarily smart and clever individual bent on your destruction?

2. Monsters will enthusiastically take some pretty extreme steps to get what they want. To play their game, you'll have to become more like them—manipulative, selfish and ruthless. Is that who you are or who you want to be? How willing are you to become more like a person you despise?

When you can't say no

All that said, we recognize that there may be times when you're going to have to deal with monsters because you have no other viable options.

In some business situations, entrepreneurs are forced to work with insensitive, callous, manipulative, ruthless people. If you need to negotiate with a monster, it's still possible to finds areas where interests overlap and both sides can get what they truly need (and some of what they want). By finding areas of alignment, monsters will use their skills and insights to accelerate results (such as closing a deal). Still, negotiating with monsters is always very hard and emotionally draining. They simply suck all of the air out of the room.

Your best approach is to remember that extreme self-importance is woven into monsters' DNA. Even the most critical and suspicious monsters are prone to see just what they want to see and believe what they want to believe—logic be damned. This may just provide you the opening to insinuate yourself into their world with minimal repercussions—if you can play to their self-importance by emphasizing their qualities that you greatly admire.

When it comes to delivering added value, monsters will often guide you to what you can do for them while crafting the illusion that you're also going to benefit. There are few times when your efforts will be rewarded. In these situations, look not for the Law of Reciprocity but rather for ways to retreat before getting decimated.

No matter the situation, it takes a lot of effort and calculated thinking to deal with monsters. Nevertheless, it can be done when there's absolutely no other choice.

CODA

Always Getting Better

In this book, we introduced the Everyone Wins Process. It's used to varying degrees by some of the world's most successful entrepreneurs, especially those who have created significant personal fortunes. It's how they move people up the business relationship hierarchy and are able to further enhance and optimize nearly any business relationship.

To recap, the underlying concept of the Everyone Wins Process is very simple:

When you help your business associates achieve their self-interests, they will help you achieve your self-interests.

You must first identify your own key goals and objectives so you're clear on what winning really means to you. Then you determine the self-interests of others by tuning in, engaging in discovery and confirming what you learn using empathy.

Armed with these insights, you look for areas where your goals overlap and for ways to support each other's objectives. This gives you two ways to get results for everyone: direct alignment resulting in enlightened self-interest, and delivering added value, which hinges on the Law of Reciprocity:

- In situations where there's the possibility of direct alignment, you take areas of commonality and frame your recommendations and requests in ways that benefit everyone. It's a win-win all around.

- When delivering added value is the way to go, you find ways to help others achieve their self-interests. This will often strongly motivate them to help you do the same.

Finally, you must track the results you deliver for your business associates and communicate to them the benefits generated by working together. You also must track the results you've received from the relationship to determine whether the benefits are adequate to continue the relationship or to enhance it further.

For most entrepreneurs who want to create great companies, becoming skilled at using the Everyone Wins Process can be instrumental. For instance, the ability to enhance and optimize business relationships is central to personal wealth creation coaching, where there's an extensive track record of helping entrepreneurs become seriously wealthy.

Ultimately, consider this book an introduction. Use it as a primer. We touched on a lot of key aspects of the Everyone Wins Process, and there is more to know about all of them. We could write erudite, extensive volumes on asking questions, empathetic responding and framing conversations (indeed, many books on those topics exist). We believe this book provides you with a strong fundamental overview of the Everyone Wins Process along with many valuable methods, tools and techniques for enhancing and optimizing business relationships.

These basics should help you become proficient in the Everyone Wins Process. In our experience, proficiency with the process is usually more than enough to further strengthen many of your business relationships and generate greater success.

In golf, for example, becoming good requires a great deal of repetition and correction. Let's say you learn the correct way to place your hands on the club and proceed to the practice range. Then, to become proficient, you must pay attention to your grip—and do so perhaps thousands of times. You'll also likely have to do a fair amount of tweaking to get the mechanics and feel just right. Of course, you can enlist the help of a professional—a golf pro—to help you refine your skills, or you can do it on your own. In time, your grip will become reliable and produce consistent shots. Yet there still will be room for improvement. Some of the greatest tour professionals in the world say that they have never reached perfection, but they're always getting a little closer. There simply is no substitute for hard work.

The same can be said of enhancing and optimizing business relationships. Many entrepreneurs who have built astounding businesses and Croesus-level personal fortunes swear by the tenets and methods of the Everyone Wins Process. And yet there's a pervasive belief among most of them that they can always improve. So even as you become masterful at helping others in ways that also further your own goals, you'll able to continually refine your abilities through practice and self-awareness.

The message: You can always get better at the Everyone Wins Process—and you are well served by always striving to do exactly that. Over time, you'll become faster and able to enhance and optimize business relationships more efficiently. This will pay off in a great many ways—from achieving your goals to helping other people achieve their objectives to being presented with a plethora of opportunities to build your business and your wealth that you'd never even imagined.

The key, of course, is that before you can get better, you need to get started. So ask yourself these questions:

Am I ready to start enhancing and strengthening my business relationships so I can do more for my business associates—and they can do more for me?

Am I ready to optimize relationships with select business associates so together we can accomplish truly amazing goals for our companies and ourselves?

Am I prepared to put in the time and effort to make all of that happen and continually hone and improve my efforts to generate huge success for myself and my business associates?

If you answered yes to these questions, it's time to make the Everyone Wins Process a part of your entrepreneurial world.

APPENDICES

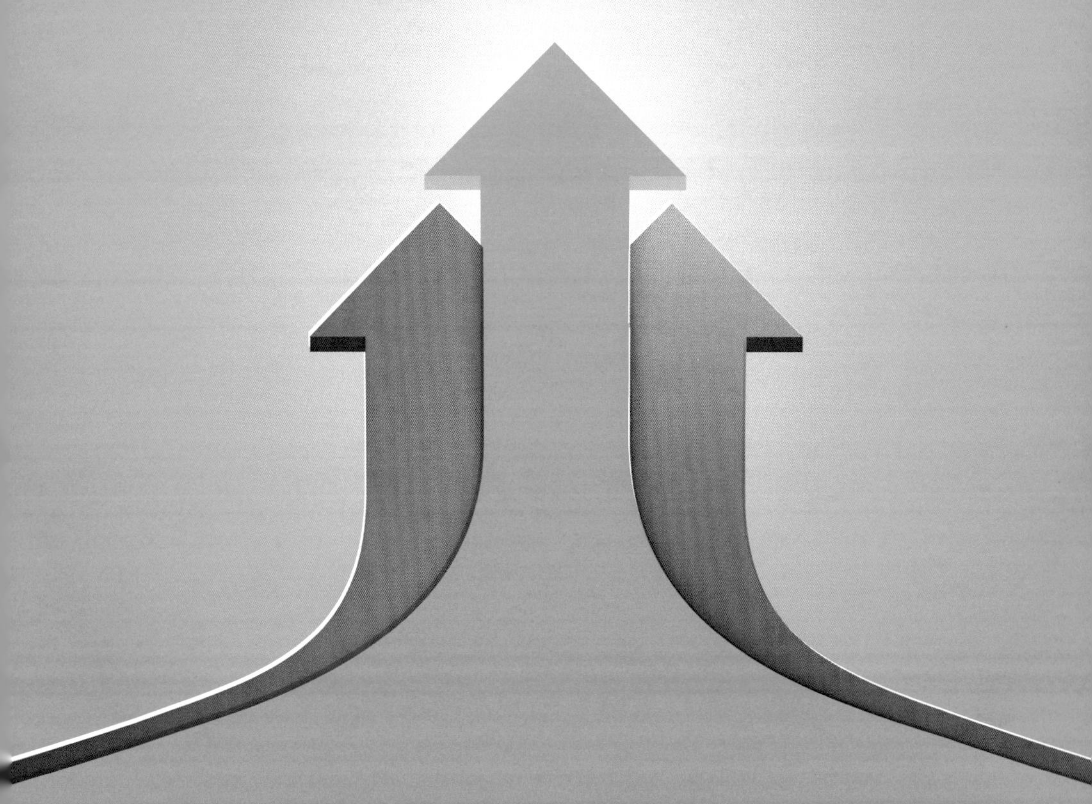

APPENDIX A

Researching Ultra-Wealthy Entrepreneurs

The basis for our conclusions throughout this book is a combination of systematic research efforts, consulting and coaching experiences, and business interactions. With respect to the research, we take two approaches.

One approach is ethnography, and the other is survey research. The former opens up a window onto the world of ultra-wealthy entrepreneurs (net worth of US$30 million or more) and also gives us great insight into their thinking, actions and most effective strategies. The latter provides data about the intentions, benchmarking and best practices of ultra-wealthy entrepreneurs. The survey research provides a way to verify and refine the insights we garner from ethnography.

Ethnographic research

The aim of ethnography is to study selected members of a society in their natural environments and produce detailed case analyses explaining both key aspects of their behaviors and the results of those behaviors. While the aim is to be as detailed as possible, this is often quite difficult because of the often arduous and complicated circumstances under which the research is conducted.

The predominant way to collect data from ultra-wealthy entrepreneurs is through participant observation and interviews. The former involves direct, firsthand observation of them engaging in various activities related to specific research questions (such as how they negotiate or how they're motivating their employees).

The other approach to data collection is structured and unstructured interviews. This can range from periodic chats to deep, involved and lengthy conversations.

Survey research

Usually based on ethnography, we focus the surveys on certain ways of thinking and acting. The aim is to validate or refine our interpretations and conclusions. It's also to get a more precise understanding of ultra-wealthy entrepreneurs.

Often the challenging and complicated part of researching ultra-wealthy entrepreneurs is building a sample. A central problem of researching wealth in any context is gaining access to knowledgeable participants. All such research either involves conducting a large-scale study where ultra-wealthy entrepreneurs are a subset or setting up purposeful samples.

With the former, there's the ability to compare ultra-wealthy entrepreneurs with those who are less affluent. This is very useful in evaluating and discerning best practices. The latter approach provides a way to develop deeper insights into this cohort.

Our survey research projects have regularly been conducted with:

- Media partners
- Organizations composed of entrepreneurs, such as business councils, mastermind groups and chambers of commerce
- Chain-referral sampling
- Introductions from professionals they have engaged
- A combination of these approaches

In effect, there's always been another party with a relationship to the ultra-wealthy entrepreneur. Working this way results in greater responsiveness—a larger, more engaged research sample.

APPENDIX B

Personal Wealth Creation Coaching

In **Chapter 1: What Is Winning?**, we said that one criterion of success used by a large percentage of entrepreneurs is becoming seriously wealthy. This is true around the world. Serious wealth is not the only criterion, of course. But it is one that is in sync with the entire concept of entrepreneurship, which is the global engine of wealth creation.

We find that entrepreneurs have varied reasons for wanting to become seriously wealthy. Habitually topping the list are being able to care for their loved ones and supporting the causes that matter to them.

If creating a sizable personal fortune is one of the reasons you've chosen to be an entrepreneur, be advised there are a plethora of experts, gurus, coaches and consultants who are available to help you become significantly wealthy. From get-rich-quick schemes pitched online to "exclusive" investment opportunities and the array of experts willing to share their wisdom on how to become wealthy (for a price, of course), there is no shortage of experts rushing in to meet the demand.

Key characteristics of personal wealth creation coaching

For the most part, these wealth creation authorities are focused on how you need to think (your mindset) and what you need to do (your skill set) in order to amass great personal wealth.

Often there are significant differences among the personal styles of the respective experts, the way the content is structured and overall approaches of the various authorities. But when we look critically at the methodologies and strategies employed by these personal wealth creation authorities (and others) who work with entrepreneurs, we see that the most successful offerings share two important traits:

1. **They all focus on helping entrepreneurs enhance and optimize business relationships.** Different personal wealth creation coaches have different ideas about how to do this, of course. Nevertheless, there's a common emphasis on strengthening business relationships and finding ways to work more productively with business associates so you excel—and become seriously wealthy in the process.

2. **They all focus on helping entrepreneurs grow and optimize their networks.** The broad methodology often starts with strategically evaluating the people in your business and personal networks. You then identify, to the best of your ability, who in your networks can be instrumental in helping you achieve your self-interests. Then you can use the Everyone Wins Process to enhance relationships as well as optimize selected business relationships.

Three scenarios for personal wealth creation coaching

Most personal wealth creation coaches take a bespoke approach based on their personal financial and business circumstances coupled with their talents and the resources of each entrepreneur client. At the same time, there are three primary scenarios for personal wealth creation coaching (see Exhibit B).

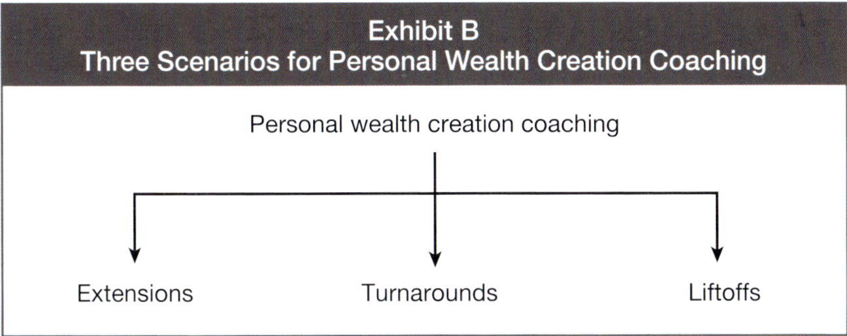

Scenario 1: Extensions

How much is enough? For some entrepreneurs, the sky's *not* the limit—it's only a starting point. Many ultra-wealthy entrepreneurs who desire to be meaningfully wealthier approach us looking for help reaching the next financial plateau.

- **Example:** A business owner worth US$500 million and seeking to become a billionaire was looking for a track to run on. His personal wealth creation coaching was strongly predicated on leveraging his key business relationships and adroitly sharing his business acumen. His ability to help those in his business relationships by putting them in touch with other business owners and professionals was the basis of the extraordinary value he was able to deliver.

- **Example:** An entrepreneur was worth close to US$200 million after selling her business. She knows she mishandled the relationships with her partners as well as with the buyer, costing her a great deal of money and goodwill. Now she wants to double her net worth by financing new firms with business models similar to the one she used with her company. But this time, her interest is squarely on how she can help these businesses and founders get results everyone wants, without any drama. Part of the solution was to get her out of her own way and sublimate her ego.

Scenario 2: Turnarounds

There are entrepreneurs who were once extremely wealthy but for various reasons lost a substantial portion of their fortunes. Now they want to regain their wealth. Entrepreneurs in this position tend to have extensive business networks, provided they didn't ostracize too many people along the way.

- **Example:** A business owner led a high-living celebrity lifestyle that both ate up his US$40 million fortune and contributed to his sending his company into bankruptcy. While he antagonized some people as he flew too close to the sun, most of his business relationships were still quite solid. His coaching involved significantly strengthening and leveraging many of the business relationships he amassed over 25 years. By carefully choosing which relationships to enhance and which to optimize, he has been able to reestablish himself and now is fast-tracking the success of his new company.

- **Example:** An artist who once rode the boom was about to declare personal bankruptcy. His coaching involved rebranding him as an entrepreneur and setting up a business catering to wealthy artists and entertainers. The goal: to maximize his extensive database of relationships with creatives and help them garner licensing deals. He has to win over individual artists or entertainers by making them see that it's all about them and helping them become much wealthier.

Scenario 3: Liftoffs

These entrepreneurs have amassed some personal wealth and don't want to stop accumulating—but they have, in one way or another, hit a ceiling and need some guidance.

- **Example:** A highly successful business owner worth around US$25 million wants to build a "great fortune" so he can underwrite research for a cure for pancreatic cancer (which caused the death of his son). His altruistic nature is working against him in dramatic ways. For example, when negotiating, he seems to lose sight of his self-interests and often makes too many concessions. The focus of his coaching is how to align his self-interests with those of the people he's dealing with and not "give away the store." This usually requires strategizing each important business negotiation using the Everyone Wins Process.

- **Example:** An entrepreneur determined he has to take some drastic action, as he is starting to run out of time and has not achieved his financial end goals. While he is well connected in his industry and his community (he knows a great many people, and they know him), he is doing relatively little to benefit from these weak relationships. Therefore, the aim is to identify the people who can help him supercharge his efforts and move some of those relationship up the business relationship hierarchy while selectively further enhancing other business relationships.

Who most benefits from personal wealth creation coaching

Not everyone who desires greater affluence is a good candidate for personal wealth creation coaching. Simply put, the best candidates have certain qualities:

- A tremendous desire to excel as entrepreneurs and become much wealthier
- The mindset, talents and skills that can be refined and refocused on what it's going to take to extend, fast-track or rebuild a personal fortune
- The desire to approach business ethically, with the aim of helping all involved to achieve their self-interests
- A fairly extensive professional and/or personal network to enhance and monetize
- Financial or other resources (e.g., brand, intellectual capital, existing businesses, etc.) that can be innovatively leveraged
- A willingness to listen and try

Caveat emptor

The upshot: There are coaches who can help entrepreneurs amass serious wealth by showing them how to optimize and grow their networks and enhance or optimize their business relationships. So if you're seeking coaching on building a personal fortune, there are professionals who can be very helpful.

That said: *caveat emptor*—which is Latin for *buyer beware*. Some "experts" are clearly charlatans and fabulists. Others are well meaning and full of good intentions, but they don't possess the capabilities or proven methodologies to actually help you. Good intentions are worthless without solid methodologies, systems and processes. In the final analysis, results are all that matter.

If you choose to seek personal wealth creation coaching to help you become seriously rich, carefully and hypercritically evaluate any professional you're considering. The right well-qualified personal wealth creation coach can prove very supportive and provide you with a tremendous education as well as a toolkit of processes and techniques that can prove invaluable in helping you create a considerable personal fortune. But failing to take the necessary steps to evaluate the professional you're considering might well lead you to purchasing extremely expensive vaporware.

APPENDIX C

Your Own Family Office

The Super Rich (people with a net worth of US$500 million or more) have historically embraced family offices going back to the sixth century, when the king's steward played a dominant role in managing the royal wealth. The modern concept of the family office came together in the 19th century with the likes of the Morgans, Rockefellers and Carnegies.

Today, the appeal of the family office among the wealthiest families is probably stronger than it has ever been. There's no business model that does a better or more efficient job catering to the needs, wants and preferences of the wealthy.

For those of us who aren't Super Rich, there's good news: Because of technology and some very ingenious professionals, new types of family offices are now available to successful entrepreneurs and others who haven't (yet) made it to the Super Rich level.

Ultra-wealthy entrepreneurs are gravitating to family offices, as are entrepreneurs who aren't ultra-wealthy but who are fast-tracking to greater personal wealth. For a large percentage of these entrepreneurs, family offices are the superior way to:

- **Grow their wealth outside their companies.** Astute investing using legally sanctioned, cutting-edge expertise is a key characteristic of high-performing family offices. While such sophistication is not always needed, it's great to be able to access it when appropriate.

- **Minimize or eliminate their tax bills.** From not having to pay taxes on such things as investment profits and the sale of their companies to significantly lowering income taxes, high-performing family offices are leading the way.

- **Protect their wealth from unfounded lawsuits**. The shrewd use of asset protection strategies is common among high-performing family offices. Using completely legitimate tools and techniques, these family offices are able to insulate wealth from litigants who seek to "steal" it.

- **Address a wide range of personal and family concerns.** Family offices are for more than wealth management. They can be instrumental in arranging for an array of family support services, including administrative services (tax compliance, bill paying), lifestyle services (concierge medicine, family/personal security) and special projects (adoptions, buying an island).

Family offices are often the best way for successful entrepreneurs to maximize and protect their personal wealth as well as help in other aspects of their lives.

Three types of family offices

Family offices are designed with one mission: *to support the financial and lifestyle needs of their wealthy family clients.* They synergistically combine elite wealth management (investment management and wealth planning) with family support services (administrative services, lifestyle services and special projects) (see **Exhibit C**).

Exhibit C What Family Offices Can Provide	
Wealth management	**Family support**
Investment management • Discretionary investment accounts • Private equity investments • Venture capital investments • Marketable alternatives **Wealth planning** • Income tax planning • Estate planning • Business succession planning • Asset protection planning • Charitable tax planning • Cross-border planning • Life management planning	**Administrative services** • Tax compliance • Bill paying • Financial statements **Lifestyle services** • Concierge medicine • Family/personal security • Philanthropic advisory **Special projects** • Adoptions • Buying an island • Overseeing the construction of a house • Acquiring an aircraft

It's not about simply having an extensive menu of expertise, however. Well-run family offices are holistic, solution-driven and structured to deliver a phenomenal experience by addressing the full range of families' needs and wants—using best-of the-best specialists.

Today, there are three major types of family offices:

1. **The single-family office.** This is the family office of the Super Rich. Each single-family office is an organizational structure that manages the financial and personal affairs of one exceptionally wealthy family. Because a single-family office is driven purely by the needs and preferences of one family, there is no standard for how it should be structured. It is designed and operated for that one exceptionally wealthy family.

2. **The multifamily office.** The aim of multifamily offices is to deliver many of the same services and products available through a single-family office to small groups of less affluent (but still wealthy) individuals and families.

3. **The virtual family office.** This type of family office is the one many entrepreneurs—including entrepreneurs who cannot afford a single-family office as well as those who can afford one but who don't want the governance responsibilities that come with it—are moving to. In a virtual family office, a professional coordinates a network of specialists on behalf of affluent individuals and families.

There is a significant yet nuanced difference between virtual family offices and multifamily offices. When we structure virtual family offices for entrepreneurs, each one is bespoke. They're cohesively customized to each entrepreneur. This difference actually makes virtual family offices more like the single-family offices of the Super Rich than the multifamily offices that work with a number of clients.

Important: Entrepreneurs do not hire virtual family offices as they would a multifamily office. Instead, a professional will tailor a unique virtual family office around them. Virtual family offices have all the "magic" of a single-family office for those who cannot afford (or who prefer not to have) a single-family office.

Do you want the best?

In working with Super Rich entrepreneurs to structure their family offices, we have seen repeatedly that they want the best—the top resources, tools and solutions—to address their financial worlds, their personal needs and wants, and the financial and personal needs and wants of their loved ones. While there are options other than a family office, presently nothing proves to be as effective in getting the results these entrepreneurs desire.

Family offices—particularly virtual family offices—are now a viable option for a large number of entrepreneurs. So you'll have to decide, when the time comes, if you want the best. If you do, then you probably want a family office.

About the Authors

RUSS ALAN PRINCE is one of the leading authorities in the private wealth industry. He regularly consults with the Super Rich, family offices and select fast-tracking entrepreneurs, and is often engaged by wealthy family members and successful entrepreneurs for personal wealth creation coaching. Prince has authored or co-authored more than 60 books for entrepreneurs, the affluent and ultra-affluent, and professional advisors to the affluent, including *Your Optimal Financial World: How Driven Entrepreneurs Can Benefit from High-Performing Virtual Family Offices.*

FRANK V. CARONE is an accomplished negotiator and one of New York City's most sought after litigators. He is Executive Partner at Abrams, Fensterman, Fensterman, Eisman, Formato, Ferrara, Wolf & Carone, LLP and is known for his creative solutions to difficult problems. Carone has attained significant achievements in both business and the legal profession. His practice comprises a diverse array of civil and criminal matters for individuals, corporations of all sizes, governmental agencies, nonprofits, professional practices and family offices, as well as high level government relations strategies. Carone's track record of producing exceptional results for clients is predicated on his ability to build powerful relationships with entrepreneurs, government officials and other professionals.

JOHN J. BOWEN JR. is the founder and CEO of CEG Worldwide, the world's leading coaching firm for financial advisors. For nearly 20 years, Bowen and his team have had the privilege of coaching elite financial advisors on new ways to deliver groundbreaking wealth management solutions to their clients while building amazing lives of significance. Previously, he worked directly with affluent clients as a financial advisor for 26 years, managing up to $2 billion in assets before selling his firm.